Fencer's Start-Up

A Beginner's Guide to Traditional and Sport Fencing
2nd Edition

Text and Photography
By Doug Werner

Start-Up Sports® **#8**

Tracks Publishing
San Diego, California

Fencer's Start-Up

A Beginner's Guide to Traditional and Sport Fencing
2nd Edition
By Doug Werner

Tracks Publishing
140 Brightwood Avenue
Chula Vista, CA 91910
(619) 476-7125
www.trackspublishing.com

All rights reserved. No part of this book may be reproduced or transmitted in any form or by any means, electronic or mechanical, including photocopying, recording or by any information storage and retrieval system without permission from the author, except for the inclusion of brief quotations in a review.

Copyright © 2010 by Doug Werner
10 9 8 7 6 5 4 3 2 1

Cataloging-in-Publication Data

Werner, Doug, 1950-

Fencer's start-up : a beginner's guide to traditional and sport fencing / text and photography by Doug Werner. -- 2nd ed. -- San Diego, Calif. : Tracks Pub., c2010.

p. ; cm.
(Start-up sports ; #8)

ISBN: 978-1-884654-77-0
Previous edition: 1997.
Includes bibliographical references and index.

1. Fencing--Amateurs' manuals. 2. Fencing--Handbooks, manuals, etc. 3. Swordplay--Amateurs' manuals. 4. Swordplay--Handbooks, manuals, etc. I. Title. II. Series.

GV1147 .W47 2010 2010934311
796.86--dc22 1010

Dedicated to
Nestor Rosario

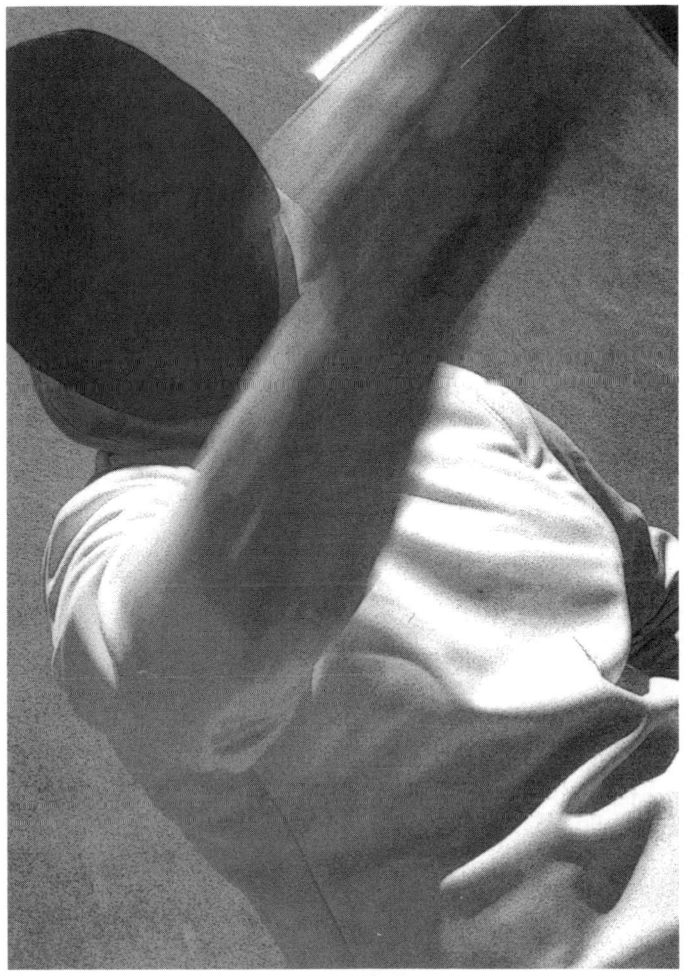

Acknowledgements

Christopher J. Reinhard
Griffin Reinhard
Maureen Reinhard

Kathleen Wheeler

Buzz Hurst

Cabrillo Academy of the Sword

Olivia Newby

Deborah B. Waldron

Dan Epperly
"Danny Green Legs"

Matt Huntley
"Van Dyke"

David Waller
"Gem Meister"

Alan Lachica
" Tattoo"

Dave Burgess
"Alaska Dave"

Mark Stanford
"The President"

Calvin Fan
Sara Allen
Eric Walker
Matt Kennel

Phyllis Carter
Lynn's Photo

Preface

It Ain't Whatcha Think

Until I took it up, fencing had always been something that was totally out of my realm. Nothing about it connected. Sure, I dug Zorro as a kid, but what he did was a lot different from what I saw fencers do on TV.

Besides, who fenced? Nobody I ever knew. It was blatantly upper crust and exclusive. Something East Coast preppie types might do. Or a jaded aristocracy somewhere in an old gray castle. It was not a growing up experience or an everyday street occurrence.

Watching the scurrying figures during the Olympic broadcasts (where else?) in their white suites with wires attached had a vague appeal (maybe James Bond fenced?), but overall looked sorta strange. Even silly. Since most of the winning fencers were European, it couldn't be hip (not to an American kid!) and the final verdict (if I ever took the time to form one) was that it was old fashioned and ritualistic. It was like watching a reenactment of an ancient battle. All these kooks getting dressed up in costumes to pay homage to something that pretty much puts most of us to sleep.

Well, guess what? It ain't like that. I have never dealt with a sport that, in reality, was so completely different from its popular image.

The fencing experience is electric! Facing your opponent with sword in hand, the adrenaline rages and crackles throughout your body like some wild beast in heat. The action is astonishing and wonderful in its *uttercompleteness* ... your focus is on the fight and nothing else. It's a heavy mind game propelled by every ounce of your energy ... all wrapped neat and tidy only to be blown to bits in one brilliant explosion after another. The skill, endurance, athletic prowess and intelligence that you and your opponent bring to the bout slam-bangs together in tiny segments of time that leaves you breathless but hungry for more.

In other words, despite it's Count Charlie reputation, fencing is an utter blast and as much fun as anything I've ever tried. It's one of the best kept secrets in sports.

My prediction: One of these days kids'll be engaging blades like they shoot hoops. In the gym and on the blacktops from coast to coast. It's that cool.

Doug Werner

Prologue

Return to the Future

As founders of Winsor Sport Fencing, we are pleased to sponsor *Fencer's Start-Up: A Beginner's Guide to Traditional and Sport Fencing* by Doug Werner. The newest addition to the *Start-Up Sports® Series* provides a vibrant compliment to our own efforts to promote participation in the sport. Our combined effort is committed to cultivating and broadening interest in traditional fencing and to promote participation in the newest of the fencing arts: Sport Fencing.

As a rule, fencing books are written by experienced fencing coaches. However, with but a few sparkling exceptions, most of these books tend to be a bit too complex and academic for the everyday person. This book is different. Like all of Doug's *Start-Up* guides, this book is written from the beginner's perspective. Doug will take you along on his personal journey into the world of fencing, from his first bewildering lessons on through to the more advanced stages of his formal instruction and training. As you learn about fencing, Doug will share his highs and lows, the good and the bad and, yes, even the comical events that make up any learning experience.

In 1993, as I began to teach my son Griffin about fencing, it became clear to me that fencing, this wonderful sport that has provided me with such fun and personal enrichment for so many years, had little hope of ever earning a place in the hearts and minds of our youth. Here in Southern California, traditional fencing was simply no competition for the many new and exciting action sports and leisure pursuits available. It was evident that if fencing was to grow and prosper beyond the 1990s, something had to change. We felt that fencing deserved an opportunity to return to the future. Fencing was too great a sport to wander aimlessly into sports oblivion.

So over the next year, father, son and good friends pioneered a new, simplified form of fencing which we now call Sport Fencing. Sport Fencing is a casual, recreational form of fencing which places great emphasis on physical and aerobic conditioning, coordination, mental agility, strategic thinking and sportsmanship. This new sport is designed to promote a spirited and controlled competition as part of the fencing experience. Sport Fencing is ideal for those seeking fun, excitement, a hearty aerobic workout and an intellectual challenge. It can be enjoyed on any open area having a level, nonskid surface, such as a gym, a basketball or tennis court ... even your backyard patio!

As part of this effort, we formed Winsor Sport Fencing to promote interest in Sport Fencing and the contemporary fencing lifestyle. Through Winsor we have developed popular educational and training materials, designed, marketed and sold our own fencing equipment and introduced an exciting line of casual and athletic apparel.

And now, Winsor Sport Fencing is very proud to present Doug Werner's new book *Fencer's Start-Up*. This engaging book will serve as an important resource and instructional tool for anyone of any age who is interested in learning more about the great sport of fencing. In addition, because fencing equipment is not readily available, we have prepared a catalog featuring Winsor Sport Fencing's dynamic new line of sports wear, specialized products and fencing equipment. To receive our new catalog call 800-713-4732 or visit our website www.winsorsport.com.

In closing, we would like to take this opportunity to salute and thank the organizations and individuals who have worked to promote traditional competitive fencing. The Federation International Escrime (FIE) and the United States Fencing Association (USFA) have played an important role to establish safety and performance standards for the sport of fencing. These standards have served as an important foundation upon which to develop the new and innovative products for Sport Fencing.

We would also like to thank Steven Paul and the entire Leon Paul organization, and the many other equipment manufacturers, for their dedicated efforts to manufacture the finest quality fencing equipment to the highest standards of safety. We salute the fencing coaches and instructors and all the fencing studios and fencing clubs who have struggled through financial hardship with sheer will and determination to keep the great sport of fencing alive. And finally, we salute Olympic medalist Peter Westbrook for the pioneering work of the Peter Westbrook Foundation, which has developed marvelous fencing programs for our nation's inner city youth.

Well, enough said. Thanks for this opportunity to let us share with you our hopes and dreams for the sport we love so much. Now it's time to begin your adventure into the fencing arts and the exciting new world of Sport Fencing.

Christopher and Griffin Reinhard

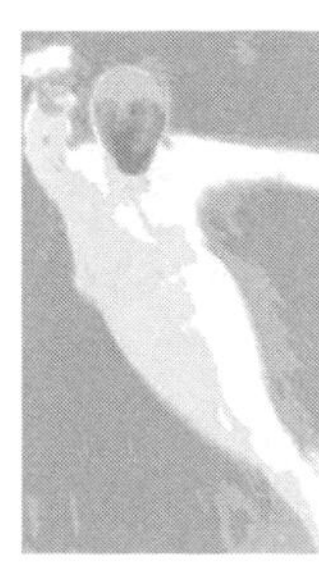

Contents

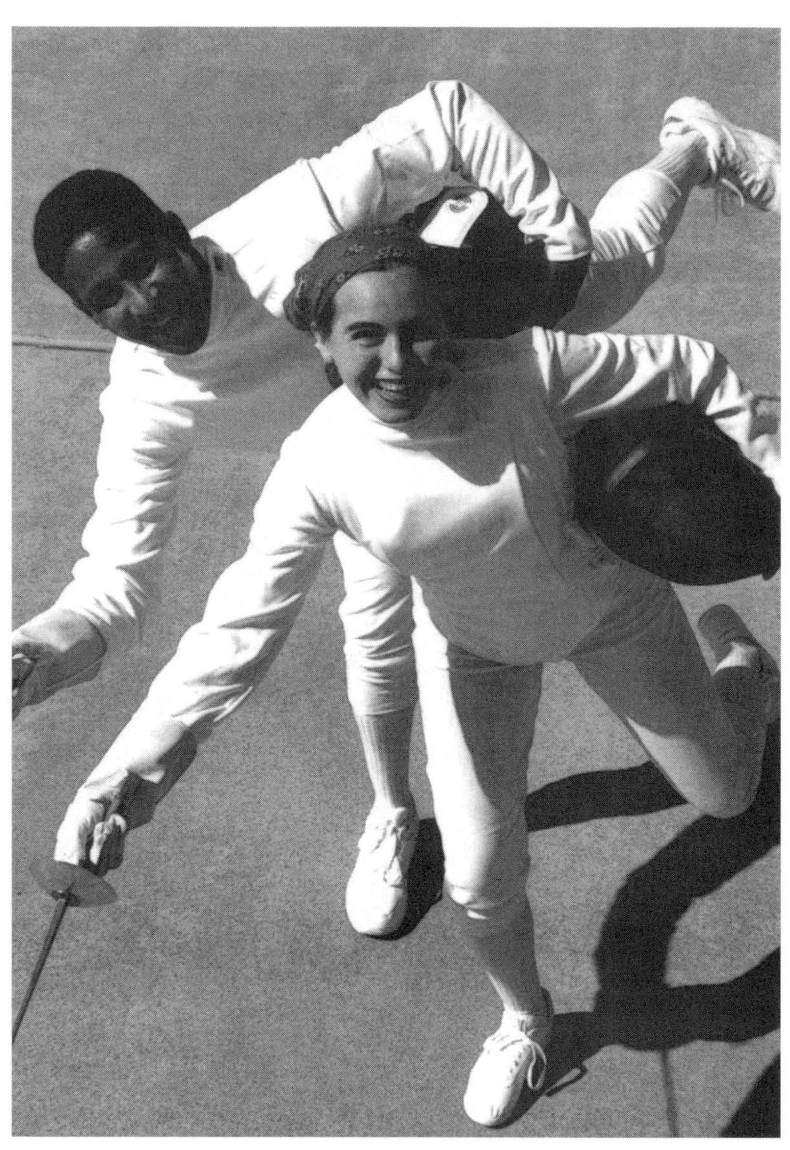

Hey! Someone tell these people that fencing is serious stuff!

You've Got to Be Kidding!

But It Looks So Weird

Watching fencers glide about looks a lot like ballet. With the feet angled the way they are, the body kinda squatty, the hand waving bye-bye and, of course, the white outfits. It's a weird picture for many of us and, as such, not very appealing. So weird that it's hard to get past.

When I announced that fencing would be the next sport that I'd explore in the *Start-Up Sports Series*, the typical response among friends and associates was a blank look or silence over the phone. You could just tell that they were seeing in their mind's eye these prancing aristocrats with pencil mustaches whipping and pointing their needlelike foils at each other. After the pause they'd chuckle and say, "You've got to be kidding, right?"

And who could blame them! I mean, really. Fencing is about as foreign to the American Middle Class (and aren't we all middle class?) as cricket.

Fencing, Anyone?

Fencing's language is incomprehensible and its image downright arrogant. *It's European for heaven's sake!* And Americans by and large do not engage in sports (or anything else!) they themselves did not invent, especially *European* sports.

But some do. And they're in it because they really dig the *romance* of the sport. The *glorious* (almost mythic) *tradition* of honor and civility. They're interested in the flair and the elitism. They like fencing because it's artistic, expressive and just plain different.

It's an *enlightened* pursuit. And like the Lexus, it has snob appeal.

Move Over Jane!

Although fencing can be arty and highfalutin (and the sport has taken few steps to change that lopsided image), the reality of it (when you're huffin' and puffin' through a drill or bout) is altogether different.

The truth is that it's an unbelievable physical workout. Imagine *Buns of Steel* times 50. After my first lesson I was drenched. I could hardly walk the next day. The last time I was that dog-tired was after a roller hockey game in August.

Aerobically speaking, it puts the video queens to shame. And to think I went into this thing thinking the physical demands would be fluff.

HA! Be prepared: No pansies allowed!

Like Pirates!

Fencing loves its tradition, ritual and glories.

There's over 300 years of it, so why not? And although all that stuff is great, on another level it sorta gets in the way. Because above all fencing is *fun.*

When you and I were kids, no one had to tell us that playing pirates was a good time. It was one of those childhood pastimes that came naturally. Like building sandcastles in the sand or playing hide-and-go-seek. Dashing around with play swords and pretending to stab each other was a real gas.

Well, fencing is like playing pirates without the play swords or the pretending. Underneath the rules and ritual, the language and the high-toned fiddle-faddle is a helluva sport. It's as exciting as bar room brawl but without the dental bills. For us gray heads it's like the little rascals revisited. It's kid stuff. With brains.

It's Not an Ax

Whackers don't win in fencing. Sheer force doesn't cut it. It's a combination of skill and thoughtful concentration that prevails. It's a physical chess game. Opponents check each other out, think ahead, set up their moves and attempt to score utilizing footwork and weapon. The sport is physical, yet outside of pure luck, scoring is an intellectual rush. It's a grand figuring-out of things.

You'll Never Fence Alone

A fencer always needs others to learn, practice and bout with. The nature of the sport demands awareness and sensitivity. Your development as a fencer requires the personal attention of other fencers. The best fencing clubs encourage open communication, civility and good cheer. They're fun places to be!

Your relationships with other fencers entail a delicate balance of competitiveness and camaraderie. As such it's nothing less than a character builder. Poor sports are not suffered for long. Conversely, the timid are brought along with a firm hand. The sport encourages it.

Fencing still forms a rather small circle in America and provides a wide and wonderful venue of opportunity. A weekend competitor can find him(her)self bouting with a national champion or even an Olympian in a given contest. Something an everyday tennis player, for example, would never be able to experience in that starry pursuit.

Fence Forever

In my classes the age span is roughly 50 years. There's a 10-year-old, a guy who's 60 and all ages in between. The sport has physical demands, sure, but nothing that most folks can't handle. The sport rewards intelligence and conservation of movement anyway. So if you're actually getting wiser with age, then fencing's the sport for you.

Everybody's Beautiful

Fencing is not a guy thing. Lots of women fence and do quite well. In fact, men and women compete with each other in many tournaments. Again, it's a sport of intelligence and skill. We're not crashing into each other here. (My use of the masculine throughout the text, *i.e.*, him, his, himself, etc. is not a reflection of bias. It's simply easier to write and read.)

The image of the thin, white Duke is laughable in a modern fencing club. Fencers come in all shapes, sizes and colors these days and can hardly be accused of being an aristocratic bunch (only in their own minds).

It's my firm belief that fencing will catch on with the mainstream sooner or later because fencing is fun, inexpensive and convenient. You don't really need the electronic apparatus to bout, so any flat non-skid surface will suffice. The equipment is relatively inexpensive, maintenance-free and lasts a long time. All the sport needs is a little push, and the nation's gyms, basketball and tennis courts will be busting with junior swashbucklers. Why not?

Humble Intentions

This book is not the only fencing book on the market. However, it's the only one out there written without the ghosts of fencing's past lurking proud and stern behind every page. The quest for basic know-how and fun is first. Tradition is covered somewhere else.

This book is not intended to replace lessons or even compete with other fencing books. It's a straightforward introduction to the world of fencing written from a greenhorn's point of view, over a span of five months and 50 or so lessons. It's pretty basic. I guess it's something of a regular guy's take on this fencing business, and if it's at all useful and amusing to you, then the author is supremely pleased.

Chapter One

Inna Nutshell

The Game

Two guys face off and try to touch the other with their weapons. The idea is to touch the other guy before he touches you. Best of five usually wins.

The playing field is a long and narrow strip, or piste (pist), 46 feet long and 6 feet, 7 inches wide. It's a forward and backward thing. You can't fence in circles or hang from the rafters like they do in the movies.

In top competition, electrical devices are used to keep track of touches and a judge or judges controls the action. Otherwise it's just the judges. When fencers fence for fun, they keep track of the hits, misses and fouls themselves as best they can.

It's a very fast game and hard to understand at first because the weapons move and hit so quickly.

In the beginning it's one darn drill or awkward foot and hand position after another. But the miracle of fencing instruction is that if you learn with conviction, it all just sorta sinks in (really!).

And then you're hooked.

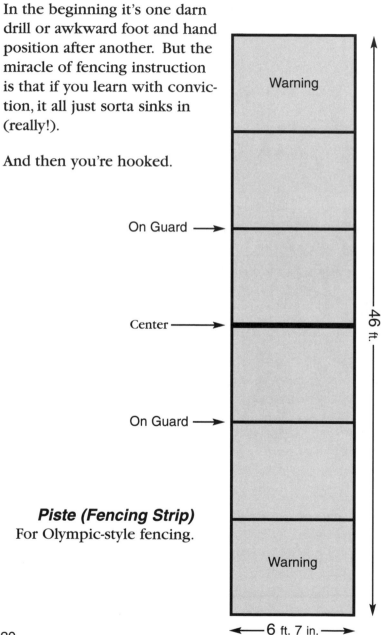

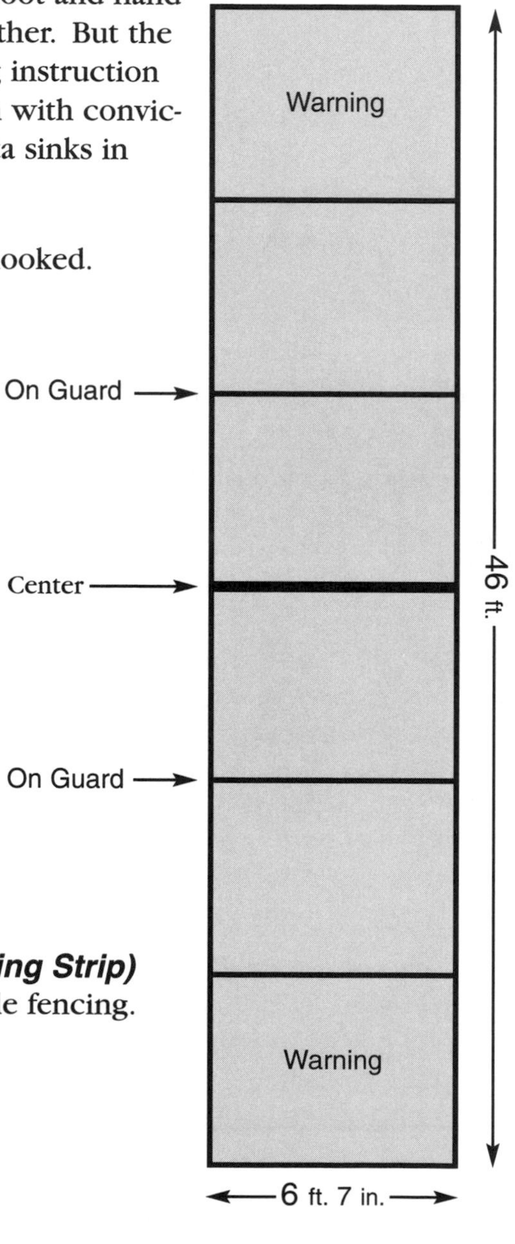

Piste (Fencing Strip)
For Olympic-style fencing.

Chapter Two

A Place to Fence

Better Shop Around!

You'll need more than a mirror and a broomstick.

A good fencing school or club will provide the facility, the instruction, the gear and the camaraderie you'll need as a start-up fencer.

Get in touch with the United States Fencing Association (USFA) to find the fencing location nearest you (usfencing.org). If there's more than one option, take the time to visit and compare. Check it out before you commit!

It's very important to learn in a place that has the goods with a group you're comfortable with. It's wise

to find a bunch that you really like because there's no getting around the need for camaraderie. Interplay is a very big deal in fencing. The instructor teaches you, of course, but the students always pair off and help to teach each other as well. That's how it's done unless you can afford private lessons. Even so, you'll want to fence with someone other than your teacher one of these days. Fencing is not a game of solitaire!

As you visit the clubs and schools, ask yourself these questions:

1. Is the place kept up?

A dirty joint is a turnoff and probably indicates something about the overall quality of the club.

2. Is the rental gear clean and in good repair?

You'll probably rent stuff at first so check out the gear students are wearing and using. Are the jackets grimy? Are the swords bent and beat? Do the masks smell like a stray dog?

3. Is everyone happy?

4. Does the instructor speak English?

Don't laugh. There are world-class fencers teaching out there who would make a New York cabbie wince.

5. Does every student stay the entire class?

Stay the course of a lesson (about an hour) and see how many "need to leave" before the buzzer. This is an excellent indicator of teaching quality.

6. Is everyone in the class occupied all the time?

If giant clumps of students are moping around doing nothing while the instructor is teaching one or two, there's a problem.

7. Is there a spirit of engagement?

This you can feel. There's a crisp feeling of endeavor in the air!

8. Do you want to be there?

The importance of finding a comfortable and friendly fencing home cannot be overstated. Fencers need other fencers. It always takes two, but to really improve you need the help of all the others, with their different styles and temperaments, in order to round out your fencing experience. You're just beginning, and there's a few months of basic training ahead of you. Choose your club or school carefully.

This is Very Important

The instructor will make it or break it for you.

Make sure you hit it off. Make sure you understand each other. Make sure it's someone you want to see at least twice a week. Make sure they know how to run a class. Make sure they know how to teach *you!*

Learning is a personal thing and fencing is a personal endeavor. Above all else, look for a teacher you trust and admire. A careless, insensitive instructor will make lessons seem like boot camp (and who needs that!). A good instructor who loves to teach makes learning fun and fulfilling (as it should be!).

I'd like to say that this book will teach you all you need to know about start-up fencing, but it won't. You'll need a good coach above all else!

Chapter Three

Basic Gear

All You Need

You don't need much in the beginning. In fact, your club or school will probably have stuff you can use or rent. Just wear sweat pants, a T-shirt and white-soled sneakers to class.

Mask

Your mask should fit comfortably and snug. No rattling around. Make sure the bib underneath your chin covers your neck. If you're interested in fencing at all, you'll buy the mask before anything else. You'll soon grow disgusted with public masks.

Jacket

The jacket should also fit comfy and snug. No loose fabric. The sleeves should cover the wrists. Too long is OK. Just fold them back.

Glove

Your sword hand needs a glove. It should fit snug, fingers to the tips. The sleeve of your jacket must tuck inside the collar of your glove.

Weapon

As a rule beginners start with the foil and learn foil fencing. It's the most popular form of fencing for one thing and many believe it builds the best foundation for learning. There are two other ways to fence and each has its own special sword. They are epee and saber.

Make sure your foil isn't too beat up, bent along the blade or unraveled at the handle.

Hand Towel

I sweat up a storm in my mask. It's hot in there! I need to towel off frequently when I'm drilling or bouting and the sleeve of my jacket doesn't cut it.

There you go.

Anatomy of a Foil

The foil is light and flexible. It can have either a straight French grip handle or a fitted pistol grip handle. The French grip is longer (the length can be used to advantage during a thrust) and can be manipulated by fingers and thumb only. The pistol grip has more of a handle to it and is less likely to be wrenched from the hand.

The French grip has been the preferred handle for

But What Should I Wear?
All you need to bring to your first lesson are sweat pants, sneakers and a smile. Your club will have everything else.

Ready to Throw Steel!
Mask, jacket and glove. The mask sets firm on the noggin, the jacket is strapped, snug and buttoned down, and the glove fits snug over hand and sleeve.

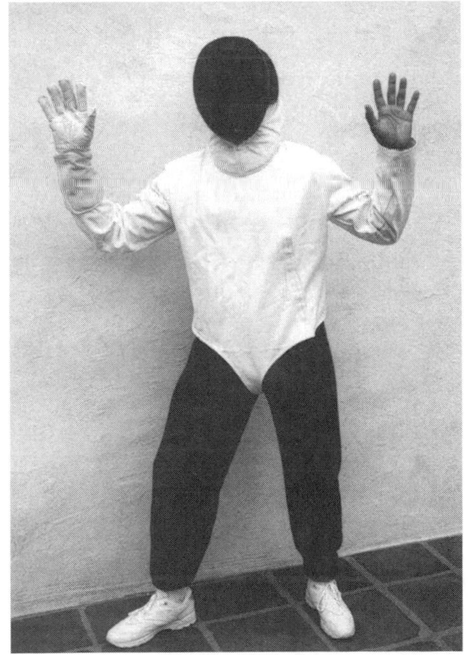

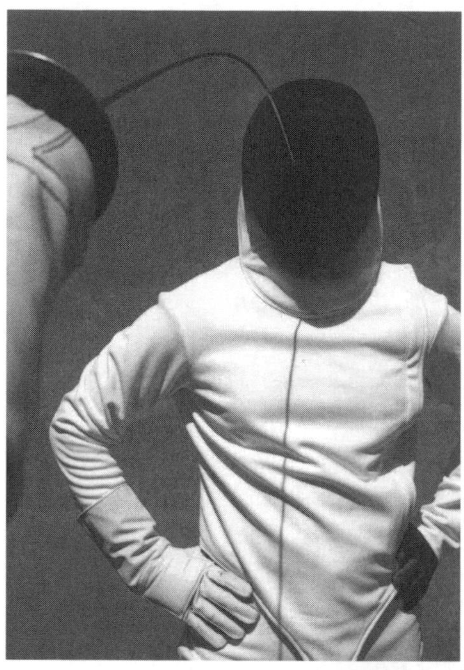

Of all your protective gear, the mask is by far the most important. Only your weapon will mean as much to you. With a mask, you'll probably never get hurt. Without it, you probably will.

It's a Tradition and a Good One. It's the responsibility of each fencer to check each other out for safe gear and proper fit.

early instruction because it demands that the fencer learn finger control. Don't sweat the difference for now. Just use what your club has to offer. Make sure you try both, however, when you have the opportunity.

The guard is small compared to the other swords in fencing (epee and saber) and separates handle and blade.

The blade has a fatter end toward the handle called the forte (fort) and a thinner end toward the tip called the foible. Obviously, the forte is stronger and less flexible than the foible and is better suited for warding off an opponent's blade.

The most distinctive quality of the ***French foil*** is the straight grip and the small guard.

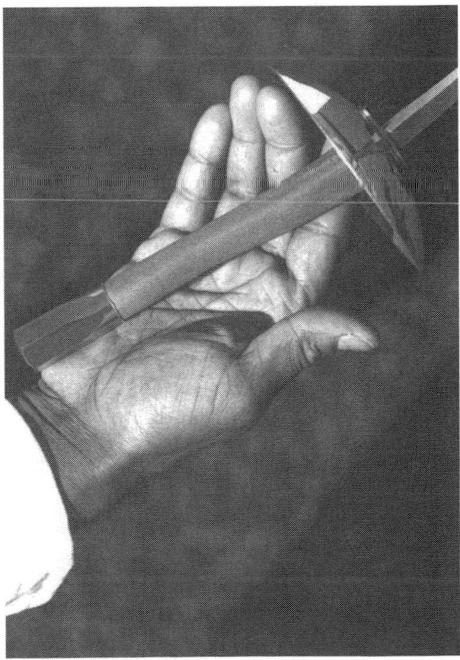

Your foil is designed to be safe.

The tip is capped by a rubber button.

The blade is ultra-flexible and will absorb the shock of even the strongest thrusts.

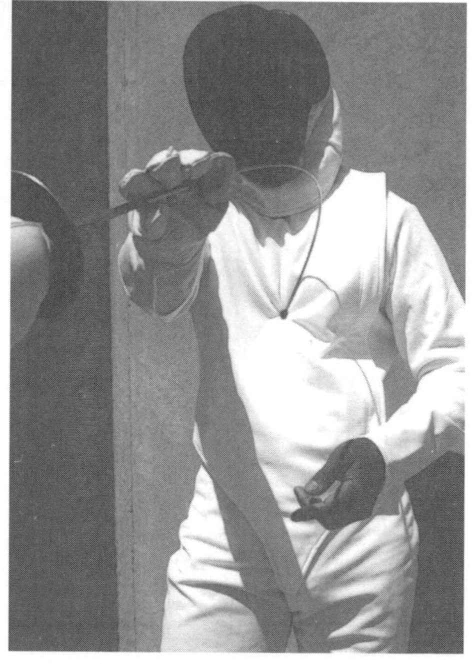

Chapter Four

Safety

Don't Worry Mom

Let's deal with the Big Question up front.

If you are using and wearing the proper gear correctly, you will not get stabbed or run through in fencing! There are no sharp points or edges on fencing weapons unless they break. All weapons have a blunt tip that cannot penetrate the jacket material or mask. Fencers no longer have to bring doctors to their fencing engagements.

There aren't even any severe pokes in fencing. The blades of the swords are very flexible. When the blade strikes, it bends and absorbs most of the force of the blow. In most cases, the heavy fabric of the fencing jacket is all you'll need in the beginning. If for some reason you and a partner are extremely heavy hitters, you can purchase specially made undershirts to protect you from bruising each other. Or simply wear more clothing underneath. It's advised that women wear plastic chest protectors and men plastic cups.

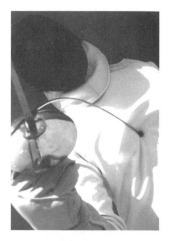

OK! What you *do* have to be concerned about is wearing the proper gear. And wearing the gear properly.

Whenever you fence with somebody or with something (like a dummy or a wall pad), always wear your jacket and mask. Even with a wall pad the blade can still break and rebound off your face or body. It does happen.

- If a blade breaks, replace it immediately.

- Make sure the bib underneath the mask covers your neck.

- Make sure your jacket is buttoned all the way and that there's no gap showing between pants and jacket.

- Wear pants or long shorts that cover the upper leg. No speedos.

- Check your mask for dents, weak spots and breaks.

- Check your jacket for holes.

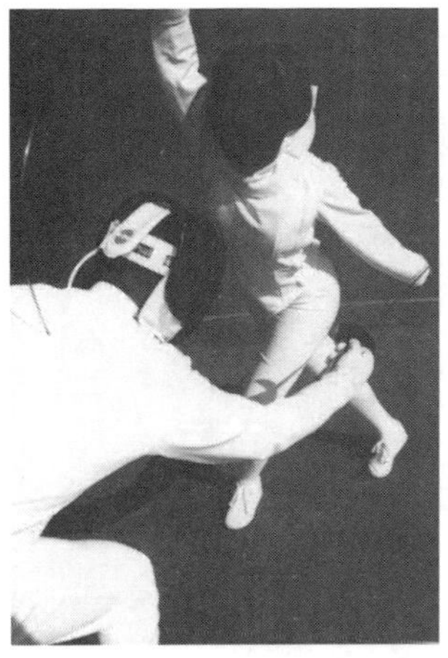

You are a fencer, not a thrasher. Fencing is a game of concentration and skillful maneuvering. Not brute force. The object of the sport is to touch your opponent with the tip or edge of your weapon. You don't pommel, whack or stab. There's little or no body contact. It's not a brawl.

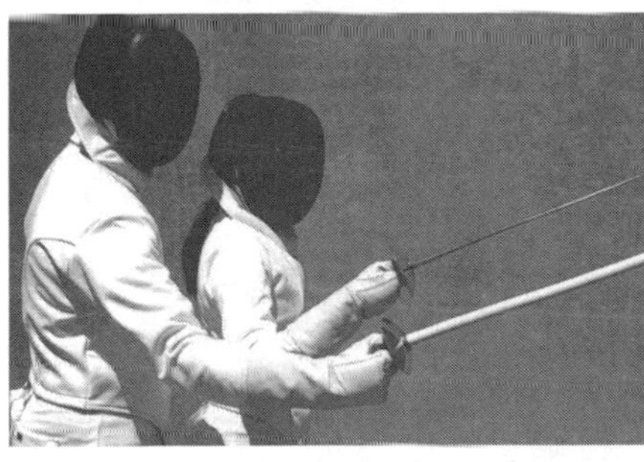

A Special Note

In order to better show blade movement, shrouds have been used over the actual blades in most of the photos. One fencer will have a white shroud and the other a black one. Without them you simply wouldn't be able to see what's what.

In some cases Olivia and Nestor demonstrate something without their masks. Please note that this in no way condones fencing without a mask.

These demonstrations are, in fact, in accord with USFA guidelines because the fencers are merely posing. Besides, since the blades are shrouded there is no safety issue.

Fencers are a Polite Bunch. They call their own hits when there's no judge ...

... and they shake hands after bouting.

Happy faces are optional. However, a wise fencer will develop good cheer in order to counter-balance the intensity of combat.

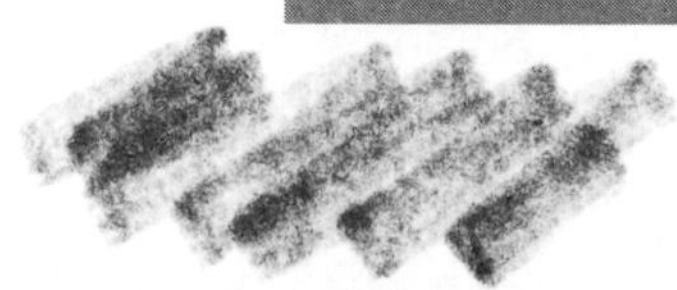

Chapter Five

About Manners

The Gentle(wo)man's Sport

Fencing was bred from a violent past. Using a rough timeline, the 16th century saw the development of the thrusting sword in Europe. Until then the sword was a heavy hacking device. The lighter weapon became part of a gentleman's attire. And apparently they used it.

Guilds of fencing masters grew throughout Europe to impart the skills of swordsmanship. These schools in turn developed fencing technique and equipment Proficiency in the art of fencing became a necessary accomplishment for the nobility and other members of the aristocracy.

Dueling became a popular method for settling legal and personal disputes because the outcome of these bouts was considered God's Will. Dueling was such a rage that at one time the gentry was in danger of dueling itself to death. Although the ritual was legally banned in England and France much earlier, it didn't altogether cease until (get this) *this* century.

Dueling gave fencing the traditions of courtesy, customs, officiating and tactics. This is where the concepts of self control and gentlemanly conduct originated. Brutality, lack of weapon control and poor manners were despised. A true swordsman was bound by a personal code of honor. This is where all that aristocratic and ritualistic behavior comes from.

The residue from those days of honor is evident in the modern game. Fencers still salute each other before they fence and shake hands after. Fencers do not argue over touches. In fact, in friendly, non-judged matches, fencers are obligated to personally acknowledge every touch received. Fencers cannot physically bully one another, swear or make threats. Heck, a fencer even needs permission to leave the strip, or fencing area.

The sport has *manners*. In this era of bellicose display, fencing seems quaint and fragile like a fine piece of china in a prison cafeteria. But it's not quaint, only a little out of time in a somewhat mediocre age. And it certainly is not fragile. Ask any fencer when their blood is up.

The Salute

Before and after bouts or lessons, fencers salute to fencing partners, judges and coaches. With feet in the first position (at right angles, heels touching) each fencer holds mask in hand and brings the weapon to his face (guard to lips, blade perpendicular). Held there for a split second, the sword is then swept down and away.

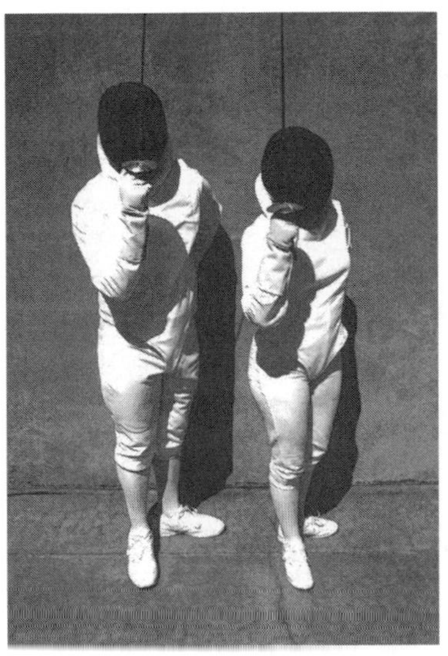

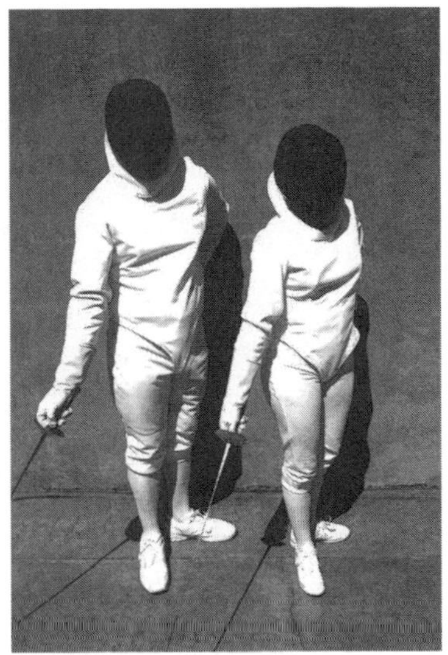

The Salute: Before and after every engagement, fencers respectfully acknowledge each other and the judge and referees if it's a bout.

No Smack Jack

Although this may be the way you *feel* after a hard-won bout, as a rule it ain't cool to rub it in.

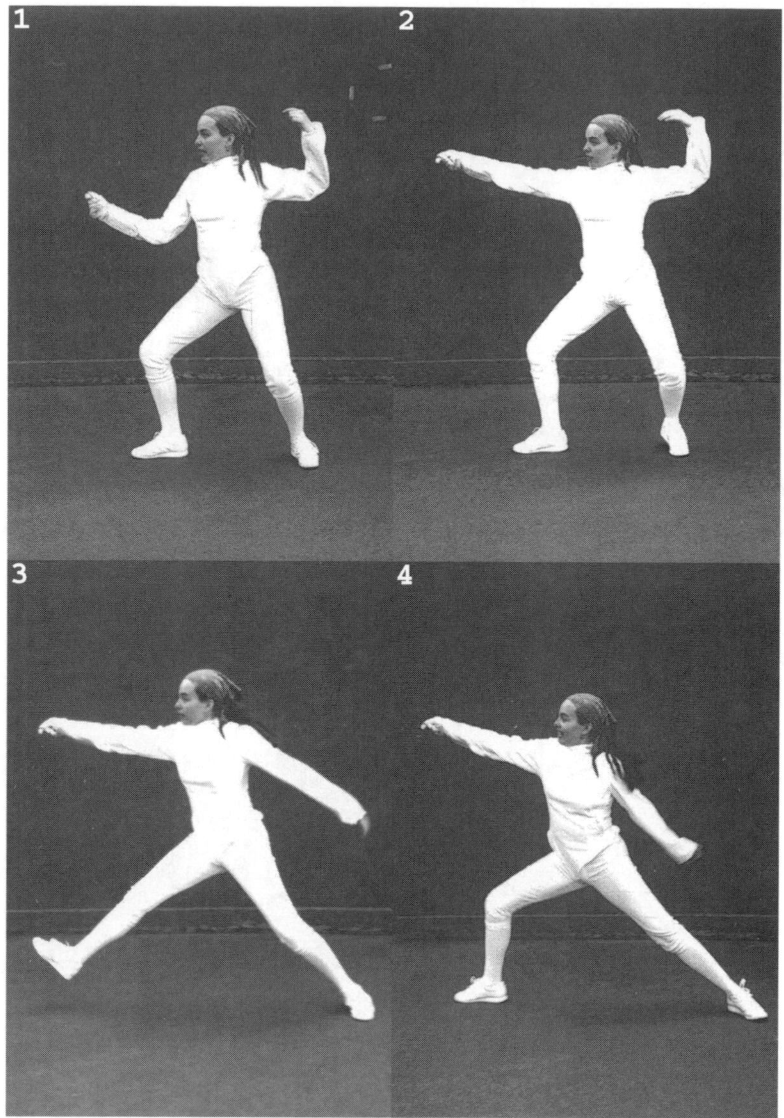

Fancy feet: The dancelike movements in fencing are as functional as they are artful. The ***lunge*** that Olivia demonstrates so beautifully in these photos is, in fact, the most lethal way to deliver an attack with a sword.

Chapter Six

Fencer's Fandango!

Moving Around

Footwork is half the game in fencing and it's pretty much the same for foil, epee and saber. The movements are a lot like dancing. To move well in this sport, you must incorporate power, skill and rhythm.

On Guard

OK, everybody knows this from the cartoons. It's the set up or the starting position. The following is on guard for foil. (There are some differences with the on guard for epee and saber, but we'll deal with that later.)

First you must determine which foot faces forward. The natural order of things dictates that right-handers fence with the right foot forward and lefties with their left foot forward.

Now stand straight. Face a target. Point your forward foot toward the target. Place your other foot at a right angle behind the forward foot, heels touching. This is called first position. (Feels just great, doesn't it. Like someone's trying to unscrew your back leg. OK, now

look at your feet. (Oh, no! You're a penguin!)

Next, step forward about a step and a half (shoulder width) and bend at the knees. Keep your torso upright and your eyes on the target. You should feel comfortably balanced, flexed and ready to go. Check out the front foot. It's gonna wanna point back in, but you gotta keep it on line.

Lift your forward arm until the hand is at breast level. Bend your elbow and point at the target. There should be a hand span between elbow and torso. Your arm is directly over your leading leg.

Raise your back arm away from the torso and bend the elbow. Break your wrist and relax your hand at about shoulder level.

This is the on guard position, or on guard. In this position you're in balance, ready to move forward or backward and at the same time ready to attack or defend.

Advancing

From on guard place the front foot forward heel-first, one step while pushing off toe-first with the rear foot. As the front foot lands, bring up the rear foot one step. Feet should just clear the ground. This is a gliding action. Watch for a bobbing head. Keep the distance between your feet. Don't end up with your feet together.

Advancing: The lead foot is always pointed straight. Push off the back foot and make quick, skimming steps.

Retreating: Push off the front foot this time and make sure you finish each step with your feet apart.

1 2 3

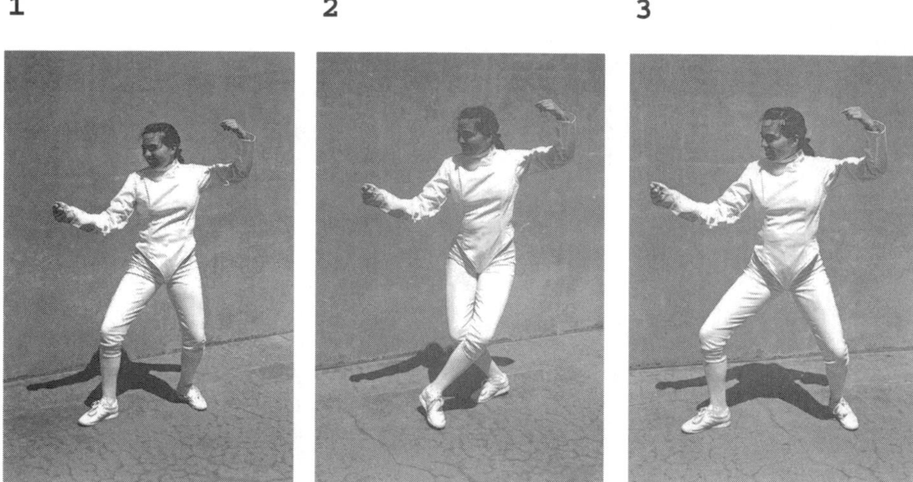

Cross-Step Forward: Like advance/retreat, no clumping feet and bobbing head.

1 2 3

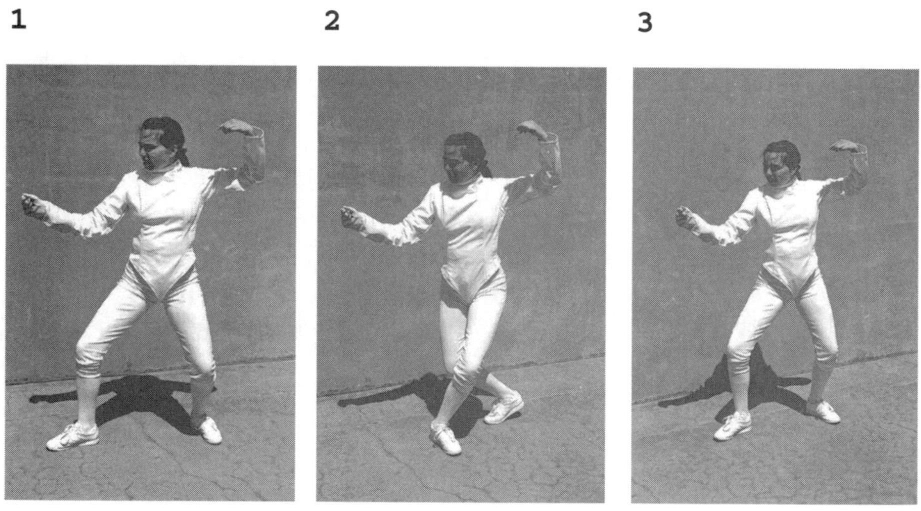

Cross-Step Back: Footwork in fencing is all about balance and maintaining a state of readiness.

Retreating

Simply reverse the advance. Rear foot glides back toe-first propelled by the forward foot heel-first. Each foot moves an equal step, thus maintaining distance. Retreating, by the way, is the number one defensive skill.

Cross-Stepping

To go forward: From on guard swing your rear foot forward and place it at a right angle just in front of the other. Immediately bring the latter forward along the target line.

To go backward: From on guard swing the forward foot backward and place it just behind the other. Immediately take that foot back along the target line taking care to maintain the right angle.

And some trickier moves:

Balestra (ba-less-tra)

This is a jumping advance with a lunge. From on guard lift the front foot slightly as before, but this time jump from the rear foot and land with both feet simultaneously. As soon as you land make the lunge.

Appel (a-pel)

This is a diversionary action. Rap your front foot sharply on the floor.

Fleche (flesh)

A very exciting and aggressive attack. The fencer leans forward over a flexed front knee until he begins to topple. Then he pushes off the lead foot so that he propels himself nearly horizontal at his opponent. The rear leg swings forward and the fencer lands on that foot.

This is an advanced maneuver and used in very specific instances. Work on the other movements first.

Practice! (prak-tiss)

How well you move will determine how well you fence. No matter how brilliant or how skillful you are with your weapon, your fencing machine needs good legs. Drill yourself through these steps until it becomes second nature. You don't wanna be thinking about your feet during a bout!

A Universal Practice Tip

Start the exercises slowly. Work on perfecting form and technique first. Then build your speed. This maxim holds true with every new fencing skill you choose to learn.

Chapter Seven

Fencing 101
Foil

Foil First

Everybody starts with foil fencing. It's universally accepted as the proper introduction to the fencing arts. It's also the most popular form of fencing. Foil fencing was designed and created for training purposes in the 18th century.

Point & Thrust

The foil is a light, flexible thrusting weapon. It's designed to score with its point on a very specific target area: the trunk of your opponent's body.

The Rule: Right of Way

In order to score, or touch, in foil fencing, the fencer must first gain priority, or right of way, over his opponent. Priority is established by extending your sword arm before the other guy does and pointing it at his target area. The other guy is totally on the defensive at this point and cannot think about attacking you until he somehow blocks or parries your threat.

Grip

How you hold your foil depends largely on the handle. In any case you never squeeze. Pretend you're holding a cute little animal. Or a golf club.

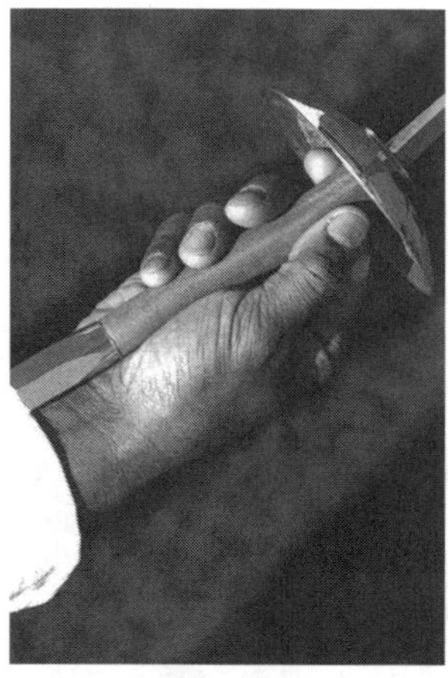

The French grip is a simple design with a slight curve. It allows for maximum finger control. Chances are you'll start with this style.

Just pick the thing up and get it comfortable in your hand. The curve of the handle will naturally fall around the palm pad beneath your thumb. What's top and bottom will be obvious. The thumb rests on top of the handle, next to the cushion and guard. The index finger curls underneath. The other three fingers act as a support. The design of this handle lets the thumb and index finger control the movements of the point of your weapon.

The orthopedic or pistol grip is built to saddle your hand. It feels secure and comfy right away. Getting the proper grip is a no-brainer. Just remember not to choke it to death.

Right of Way: Priority goes to the fencer with the extended sword arm.

On Guard: Ready to retreat or ready to attack. Flexed, in balance, in gear.

From
on guard ...

1

... Olivia extends
her sword arm,
makes the
thrust ...

2

... and executes
the ***lunge.***

3

On Guard With Weapon

In on guard, turn the sword hand palm up with the handle pressed slightly into your pulse. Bring the elbow out a bit so that the point of your foil slants in and not straight out. Your hand is about breast level and the tip of your weapon is eye level.

You're now in on guard with a weapon. You should be flexed, in balance and ready for action. Everything should feel comfortable except for your aching sword hand (which no doubt has never been contorted like this). Unfortunately, there are more contortions to come, so buck up. You'll get used to it.

Thrusting

From on guard simply extend the point of your foil by extending your arm straight out from the elbow. This is how you begin every offensive action. Without it you have no right of way and no right to score.

Lunging

Simple yet not so easy to execute and to get right every time. This is *the* offensive action. Most of your hits will involve the lunge.

From on guard, extend your weapon at a point in space. Then execute all these things at once: kick straight out (not up) with your lead foot, drop your rear arm straight back along your rear leg, straighten your rear leg, keep your rear foot flat on the floor and your posture upright (not leaning forward). And keep the point of your weapon on target throughout.

Yes, it's a lot. But it's a good bet that much of it will come naturally. You'll only have to worry about a foot that angles, or an arm that doesn't drop or a foot that doesn't stay flat. It's something you need to drill and practice until you die. You'll get it soon enough and perfect it over time.

Hitting a Target

Your club or school will have pads on the wall and/or a dummy to practice your touches with the point of your foil. Otherwise, simply hang something soft, yet firm and durable on the backyard fence. Carpeting works.

There is definitely a technique. Start with your thrusts. Stand close enough to the target so that you can hit it by simply extending your weapon. As you touch, lift your grip. This will ensure that the blade will curve up when you hit and not (awkwardly) down or sideways. Don't stand so close that the blade really loops. Determine a distance that will result in only little blade benders. Actually, that's also how you want to hit real opponents. Determining your touching distance will be very useful latter on.

After you get the hang of the hit with a simple thrust, start in with the lunge. Again, you'll want to carefully judge your lunging distance so that you don't warp your blade.

Valid hits or touches in foil must be thrusts that strike solidly with the point of the weapon. Touches aren't valid if they land along the flat of the blade.

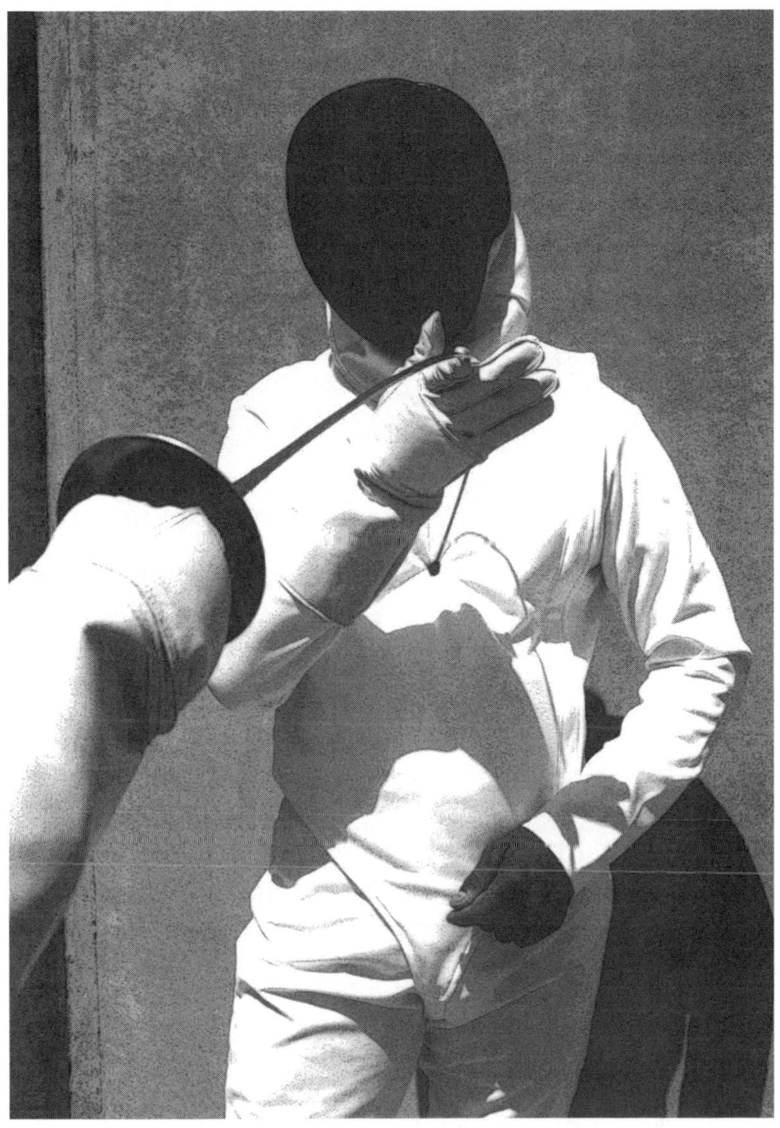

Making the Touch. Push up a bit on the handle to make the ***C curve.***

To find your ***fencing distance***, first ***lunge*** and make the touch ...

1

2

... then ***recover*** by stepping back into the on guard position ...

3

... and take another step back.

Distance

Your proper fencing distance, the distance between you and your opponent, is equal to the length of your lunge plus a step. To determine your fencing distance, face a target in the on guard position and extend your weapon so that you achieve a slight bend in the blade. Slide your rear foot back and assume the lunge position. Without moving the rear foot, recover back to on guard. Then take a step back. Note the distance from your target. This should be your fencing distance. Try a few advance lunges from this spot and fine tune your location.

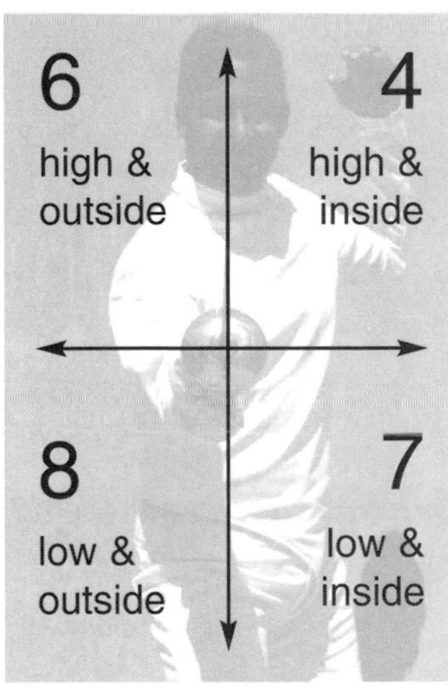

Lines

The target area of a foil fencer can be divided into four simple parts or lines. Intersecting at the foil hand of a right-handed fencer, the parts (or lines) stretch to the fencer's upper right (high outside), upper left (high inside), lower right (low outside), and lower left (low inside). In the same order, these areas are numbered 6, 4, 8 and 7.

Got that? It's confusing because we're skipping numbers, lines aren't usually thought of as parts and the whole ball of wax smells scientific and, therefore, (unnecessarily) convoluted. But there are ways to make it simple: Just memorize the number to the part and know that the parts are called lines. Heck, just look at the picture real hard.

It's very important to get this because that's how you map things out in this sport. It's how you find your way around.

Foil Overview

You'll get over the sound and fury of blazing swordsmanship rather quickly.

When you first fence, it's a blur of crashing blades. Whack! Whack! Whack! You'll think, *Man, I gotta hit that guy!* And in the land of fencing ignorance, the custom is to see who can swing the most and the meanest. Granted, it's alotta fun, but it's not really fencing. Like two little boys duking it out in the yard, it's a windmill approach where skill and tactics give way to excitement and fear. If an attack lands, it's pure happenstance.

Soon enough you'll discover that fencing is a game of skill and reflexes. It's a real rush to make a skillful touch or a clean parry against one of your peers. You'll feel like you've earned something. Heck, it's a lot more fun to know what you're doing!

On another level you'll discover that fencing is also like a poker game. Bluffing is a very big part of it. Players lay out the traps and try to draw each other out. If both fencers are highly skilled, it's the mind game that starts to matter more and more. Fencing well at that point is very sweet.

In the beginning it's so much bashing away. It's fun, but inconclusive.

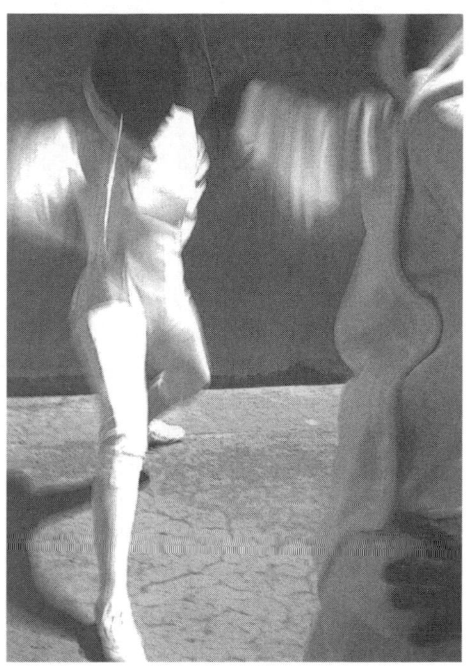

Scoring the clean hit is the real rush. Especially if it's one that took a little setting up to accomplish.

The 6th Position

Views from head-on and over the shoulder.

The 4th Position

The 6 and 4 will take you a very long way.
Just get these two down for now.

In order to control the bout, a fencer must know his opponent. He must analyze his movements and look for patterns. Always searching for the weaknesses that can result in the open line.

Of course, he must realize that the other guy is doing the same thing, and that he's gotta keep his eyes peeled for the surprises.

As you practice, avoid drilling the drill. Mix it up. Watch your partner and keep track of his every move. Learn to defend and counter the real action. Think and fence beyond the drill and the clash of engagement.

Defense

He attacks, you attack and there's defense in between. After all, this is a combat sport, and you have to know how to protect yourself. You'll discover soon enough that defense is sort of a prelude to offense. After a successful defense, a good fencer immediately goes offensive.

Parries

How to Hold the Positions

Guarding these parts (or lines) requires a special position for the foil, foil hand and foil arm. The 6th position (see opposite page) you already know. It's the position you assume in on guard. The pictures show better than words how to hold the foil in all four lines. All these foil/hand/arm positions are designed to ward off, or parry, an attack by an opponent.

This is where fencing gets weird (if all that stuff about

lines didn't already do you in). The required hand and arm contortions are simply impossible to execute comfortably at first. The low line positions in particular (7 and 8) are unlike anything you've ever done or seen in the natural world. It's something that you can do, of course, but getting it right will take time (hey, I'm just being honest.)

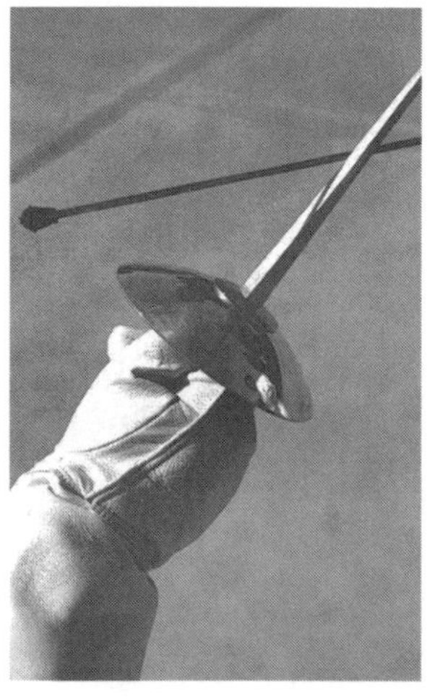

A couple notes about blade blocking (parrying):

1. A defender wants to use the fat part (forte) of his blade against the skinny part (foible) of his attacker's blade. Fat versus skinny wins.

2. Parries are best executed with smooth and concise movements. The more you swing about, the more target area you'll need to protect. Actually, this smooth and concise stuff is where it's at with all aspects of swordplay. No swoooooshing swings!

Lateral or Direct Parries

These are simple blocks or parries going between 6 and 4 in the high line, or 7 and 8 in the low line. The defender must move his arm to complete these parries.

Circular Parries

These are parries made with the fingers and wrist only. When the attacker circles underneath your blade (disengages), you can block his blade by circling around his and reengaging his blade in the original position.

The 7th Position

This and the 8th are your low-line positions.

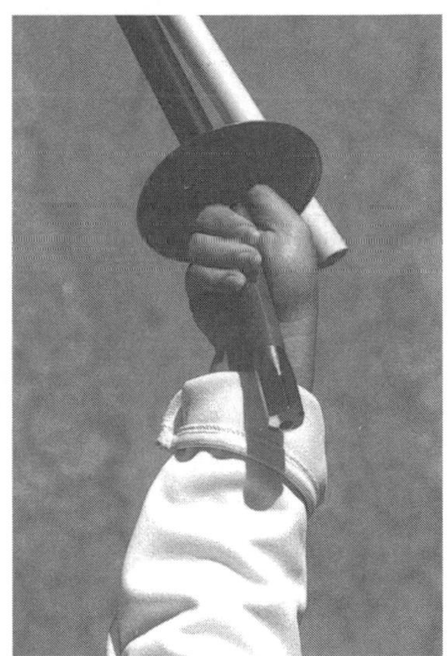

The 8th Position

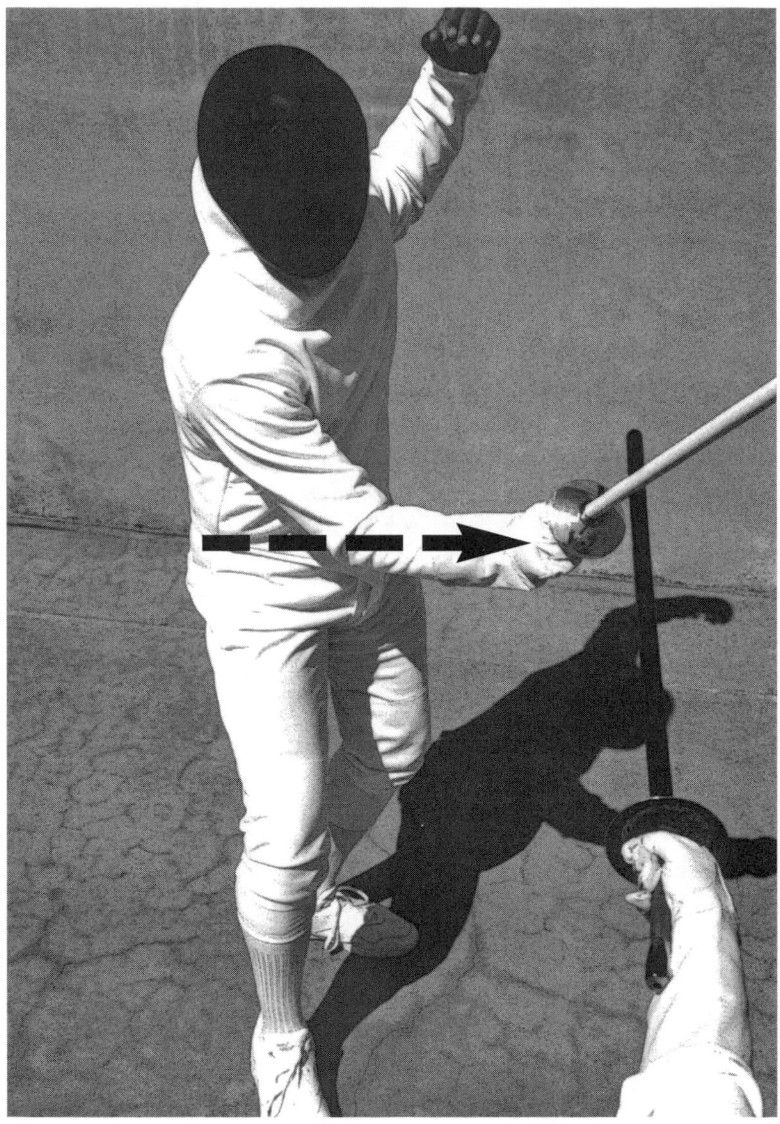

The ***direct*** or ***lateral parry*** is the most common parry and the one you'll use the most in the beginning. Above, Nestor has gone to the 4th position from the 6th in order to block an attack in that line. The action is a sharp horizontal arm movement. It's used between 4 and 6 (as shown) as well as 7 and 8.

Semicircular Parries

These are parries that entail traveling in an arc between 6 and 8 in the outside lines or between 4 and 7 in the inside lines.

Diagonal Parries

These are parries that sweep in a diagonal line between 6 and 7, or 4 and 8.

Don't Just Stand There!

Fleet and confident footwork will get you out of more hot water then nifty swordplay! When the other guy is charging in, it's important to backpedal as well as block. Don't grow roots!

There is no glory in standing your ground. Besides parrying the attack, you must think distance. After all, he cannot touch you if he isn't close enough. And you need the distance to prepare properly for your own offensive.

Think of distance as a real thing and not only empty space. Work it like your feet and your weapon!

Drills

You definitely need a partner to practice the parries. You can use a dummy with an arm, but there won't be the response and the give and take that is so much a part of this sport.

Despite the ugly images the word "drill" brings to mind, drills aren't necessarily boring or rote. First, it's a great workout if you're doing it right. Second, you're fine tuning a technique so there is some thought and focus required. Third, your partner can mix it up (as he should!) so that you're not merely drilling the drill. At any rate, the only way to get this material down is to go over it, accept the feedback of your peers and instructors and let it soak in over a number of repetitions.

He Scores! Offense

Before the offensive action can be valid, priority must be established by extending the foil at your opponent's target area. If the action is taken after your opponent's attack, that attack must be validly parried first.

The concept of priority is what marks foil fencing. There is no room for a wild, charging style that cannot defend itself. Your hits will be invalid. You simply won't score.

Simple Attacks

There is one direct attack. The rest are indirect attacks. Indirect means you change the line before the thrust.

Straight Thrust

This is usually a lunge into an unguarded section, or line, of your opponent's target area. This is the direct attack. There are no embellishments. You see the opening and attack!

Disengage

An indirect attack in which you pass your blade underneath your opponent's blade and lunge.

Cut-Over

An indirect attack in which you pass your blade over your opponent's blade and lunge.

1 2 3

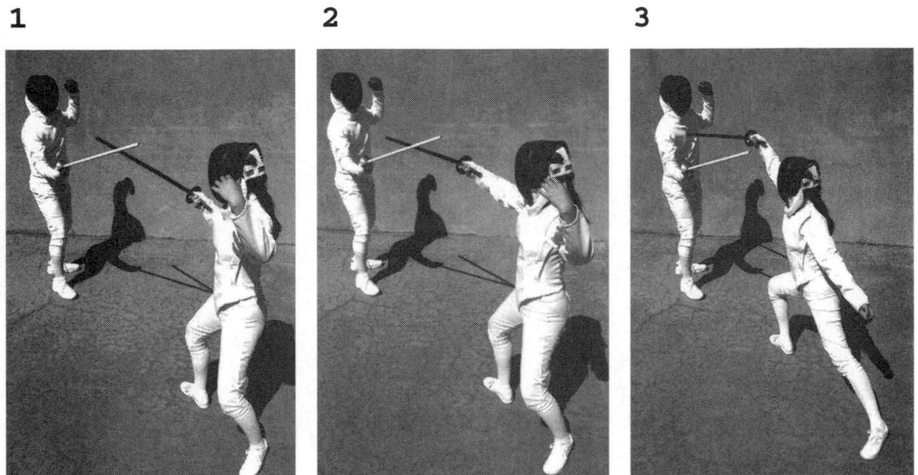

Straight Thrust: Offensively, this is your bread-and-butter shot. Olivia sees the opening and makes the ***simple attack.***

1 2 3

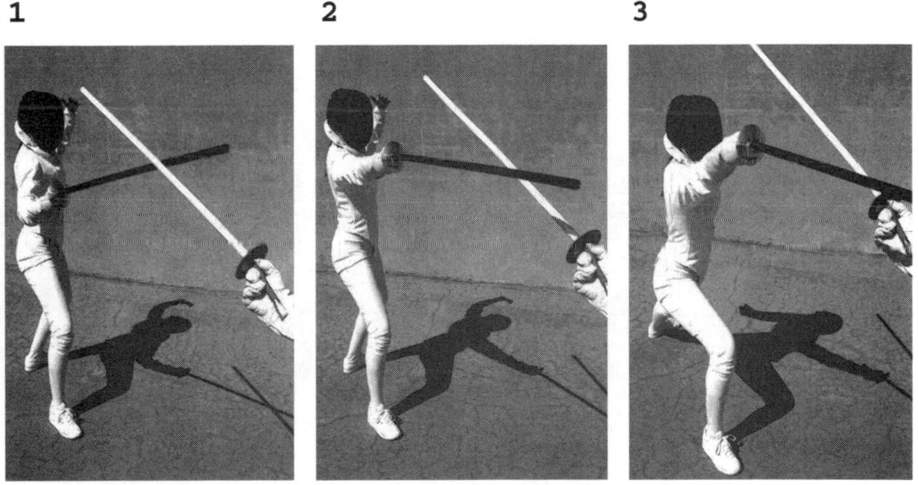

Disengage: This and the cut over are among the most common ***indirect attacks*** and blade movements. Olivia simply passes her blade underneath Nestor's and lunges into the open line.

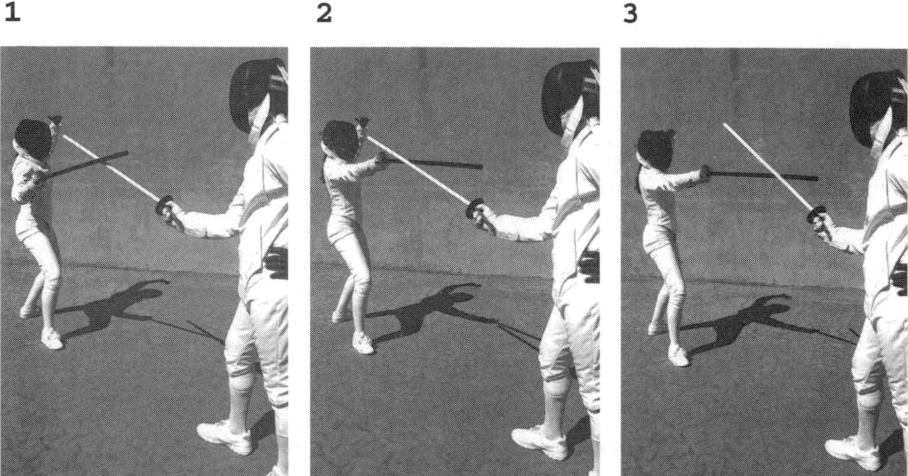

One-Two: One of the most common ***compound attacks***. From on guard, Olivia ***disengages*** and fakes an attack (***feint thrust***) in one line. This draws a parry attempt by Nestor.

Olivia ***disengages*** again (back into the original line which is now open) and makes the successful lunge attack.

Beat Attack

An attack in which you slap, or beat, your blade against your opponent's blade and lunge.

Mixing It Up: Compound Attacks

Combinations of two or more actions executed in succession are called compound attacks. The final action is the thrusting action, and the actions before that are called preparations.

Common Preparations

Feint Thrust

This is a false attack intended to draw your opponent into a desired response or parry attempt in order to open a line for the actual attack. The attacker extends his foil arm and aims at a specific target. It must look like an actual attack to achieve the desired response. The action after a feint is usually to disengage into the newly opened line.

Beat

The attacker slaps his blade against his opponent's blade, either opening a line for an attack or coaxing a beat in return, around which the attacker disengages or cuts over to make the hit.

Press

A subtle version of the beat in which the attacker applies pressure to an opponent's sword in hopes to elicite a press in return. With the return press, the attacker springs a disengage into the open line.

Common Compound Attacks

One-Two

The attacker makes a disengage and makes a false attack into the newly opened line. If the defender uses a lateral parry to block the feint, the attacker circles back underneath the parry into the original line and makes the hit.

Double

Again, the attacker makes a disengage and makes a false attack into the newly opened line. If the defender uses a circular parry to block the feint, the attacker circles the parry, traveling in the same direction as the disengage, and attacks into the open line. This circular attack is also called a corkscrew (a much better name!)

Riposte (Rip-ost)

This is a fancy French name for an attack made after a successful parry. Like the attack, a riposte can be simple or compound and can be made in any line. The idea is to riposte after every parry. You don't just stand there and block attacks. Think parry/riposte!

Ripostes you make after the first one are called counter-ripostes.

Drill, Drill, Drill!

Obviously, at this point drilling partners are practicing defense and offense. While one guy is drilling his doubles, say, the other guy is working on his circular parry.

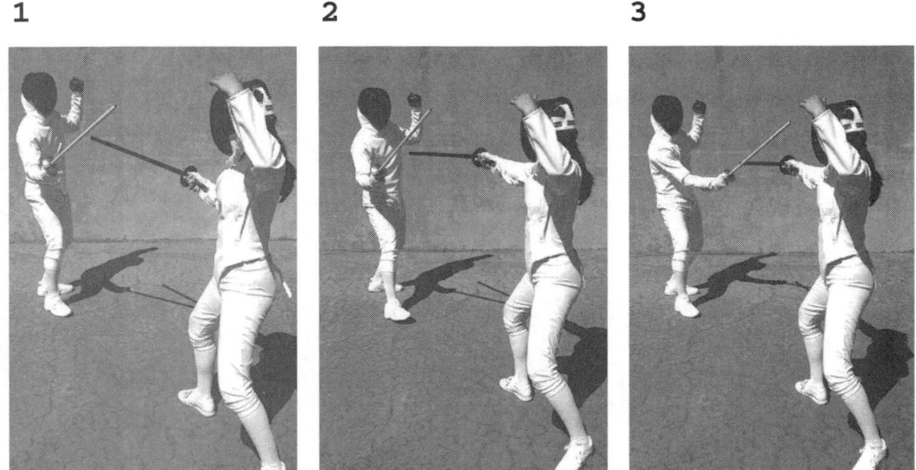

A conversation between blades. From on guard, Olivia makes an ***attack*** from which Nestor ***retreats*** and ***parries.***

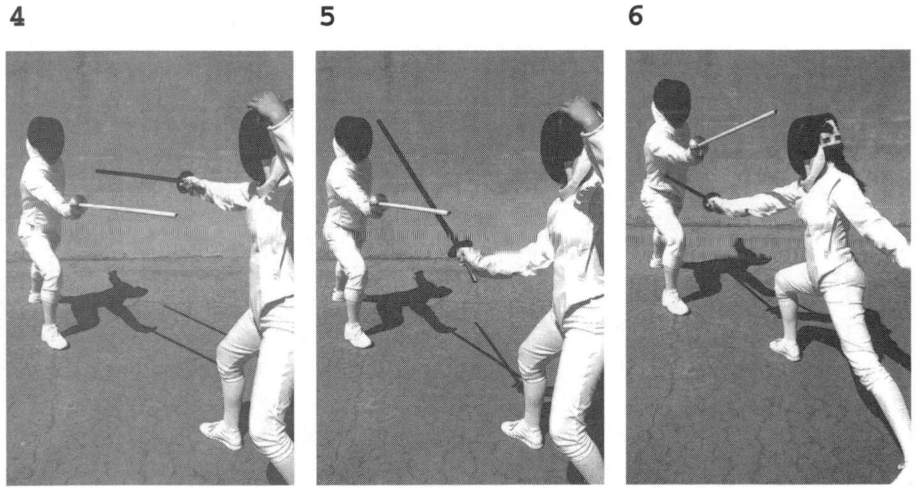

Nestor makes his own threat with a ***riposte.*** Olivia ***retreats***, makes the ***parry*** and attacks with a ***counter-riposte*** which is successful in part because Nestor didn't retreat soon enough. As you can surmise, this can go back and forth like Ping-Pong if both fencers are careful with distance and skillful with their parries.

1   2

There are shades of differences among the various ***attacks on the blade***. In pic #2 the action could be ...

3   4

... a sharp slap for a ***beat***, a push for a ***press***, a slap and push for an ***expulsion*** or a grazing action for the ***coule***. Whatever it is that Olivia has done, the line is open and Nestor is shish kebab.

Keep At It!

You learn through repetition after repetition. The mind doesn't always get it, but the muscles will. Muscle memory takes over after awhile and you simply start doing it. It sounds sorta spacey, I know, but that's exactly how it works if you drill with concerted effort.

Try to understand what these *actions* can do for your game. Don't let the weird *names* for things trouble you. (You're not alone! Words like froissement and prises de fer are downright frightening for everyone except language majors and diplomats.)

Don't think you have to get it all at once. Most fencers have only a few moves in their fencing quiver. Acquire stuff as you see fit. Make sure that what you do use, you use well.

More Foil

Preparations

These actions prepare the way for the final action: the hit.

Attacks on the Blade

We've covered some of these. An attack on the blade will either open up a line for a direct attack or draw a response around which you can make an indirect attack.

Beat: A slap on the blade.

Press: A push on the blade.

Expulsion: A slap and push on the blade.

Coule (koo-lay): A graze down the blade.

Derobement

This is the defense against attacks on the blade. Basically you're evading the attack with deft finger action. It takes perception, focus and quick reflexes to avoid such actions.

Takings of the Blade *or Prises de Fer (pree-de-fair)*

As the name implies, these actions can put you in control of the other guy's blade. These moves are particularly cool. It's like the offensive action has a built-in defense.

Bind: Taking the blade diagonally from a high to low line or visa versa.

Croise (kwa-zay): Taking the blade from a high to low line or visa versa on the same side.

Envelopment: Taking the blade and finishing in the original line of engagement.

Counter-Attacks

Stop Hit: This is a counter-attack into an attack. Stop hits score only if they're made before an attacker's final action.

Stop Hit in Opposition: This is a counter-attack into an attack that deflects the blade.

Defense Against Counter-Attacks

To defend against the counter-attack, a fencer must speed the delivery of the final action or parry.

One of the coolest tricks in fencing is the ***bind***.

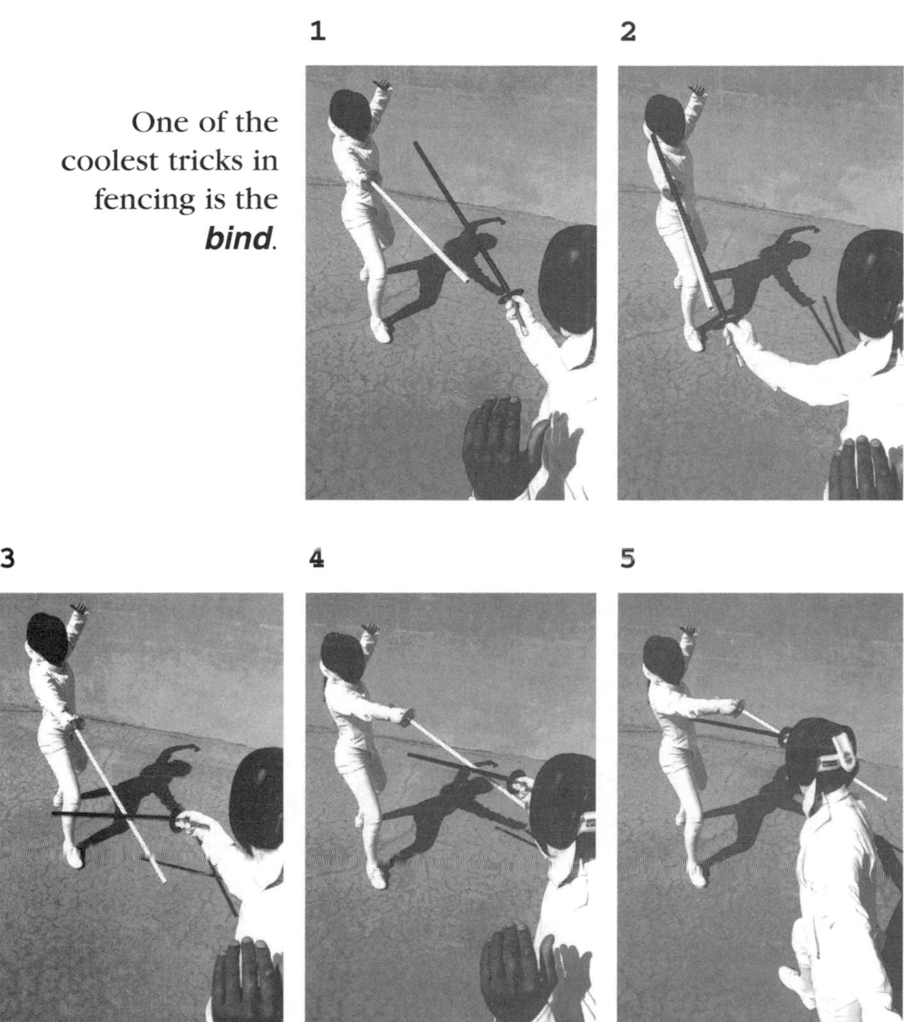

It's a ***taking of the blade*** action that starts out as a defensive ploy, literally wraps up your opponent's sword and sets him up for the score. The idea is to catch the other guy's weapon while his arm is extended. You also want to use your forte against his foible to gain additional leverage as you wrap him up.

A Big Target
You can score anywhere on your opponent in epee. And because there is no right of way, it makes for some very cautious fencing.

Waiting ...
It's not uncommon for epeeists to stand pat like this for quite some time.

Doink!
Each is waiting for the other to make a move and thus expose themselves to attack.

Chapter Eight

Anything Goes!

Epee (ep-ay)

The epee is a descendent of the rapier, the dueling sword used in the 17th century. It's application is the closest thing to actual dueling among the three fencing weapons.

It's a Little Different

The Tool

The epee is heavier than a foil, has a larger guard and has a stiffer blade. The latter is attached a little cockeyed in order to reach out and touch those hard to hit spots (like the other guy's sword hand). Like the foil, the epee is a pointed, thrusting weapon and hits are only valid with the point.

BIG Target Area

Unlike foil, your entire body is a valid target area. That's everything: head, hands, feet and torso.

No Right of Way

Unlike foil, you don't need priority to score. This means scoring comes fast and furious. Even simultaneously.

Tie Scores Count

Simultaneous hits are considered double touches. Each fencer gets a point. This can really mean something if one guy only needs a point to win and his opponent needs two or more.

Very Fast

Hits are scored by time difference. A fencer's touch must land 1/25 of a second faster than his opponent's in order to win the point. Touches made within 1/25 of a second are considered simultaneous. Since the time margin is so critical and the action so fast, epeeists use electric weapons to keep track of scoring.

Epee Basics

Grip

The grip is the same as in foil fencing.

On Guard

The on guard is very similar to foil except the sword hand extends a bit more and is positioned behind the guard to protect as much of the hand and arm as possible.

Hits

Hitting or making the touch is much the same as foil except that the wrist is used more to place certain touches, especially those that need to figure around the opponent's guard.

No right of way makes for numerous ***simultaneous hits.***

Hitting in angulation is big in epee. The weapon is built for it.

On Guard: The trick is to hide behind the huge bell of your weapon's guard.

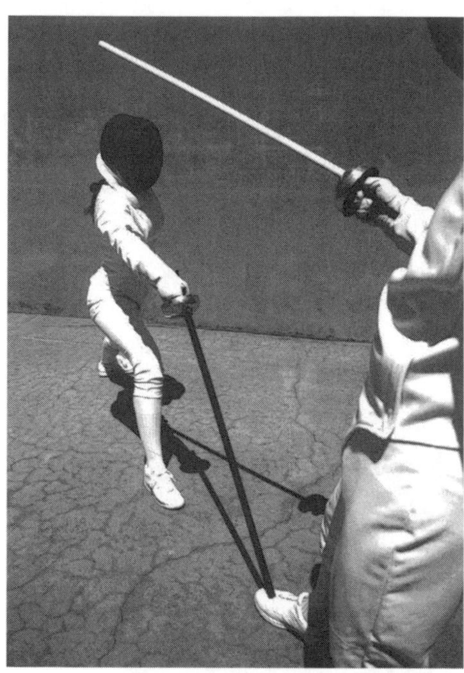

Quick and accurate point placement is an important skill to develop in epee ...

... as well as ***taking the blade*** and ***hitting in opposition.***

Footwork

Footwork is the same as foil except that epeeists will sometimes advance by moving the back foot first and retreat by moving the front foot first. This all goes back to the extended target area in epee. Epeeists are very careful about fencing distance and sticking a foot or knee out too far where it can be easily touched.

Epee Overview

It's always risky to attack the body because this exposes the epee hand and arm to a counter-attack.

Epee demands accurate point placement. Wrists, hands, feet and arms are small targets and hard to hit.

Tactics are dictated by the large target area. Epeeists must use the guard to protect their forward target areas (weapon hand, wrist and arm). Any movement of the weapon arm from on guard will expose them. The tactical solutions are to take the blade (the offensive action) or to make short and fast attacks to a forward target.

The safest way to score in epee is to take an opponent's blade during the attack and hold it off target while making the hit.

Epeeists defend against taking of the blade by slipping off, hitting the opponent and moving away. Or by avoiding the taking of the blade and hitting him while he's finding your blade.

If you fail with an attack, it's safer to continue the attack with a straight arm in opposition (your opponent's blade deflected) than it is to parry back and forth with a bent arm. Whether continuing the attack or parrying, it's better to keep the arm straight and protected by the guard.

Epeeists are allowed bodily contact so you must be prepared to deflect against strong opponents. Epeeists must also know how to fence in close quarters.

Defense

Using the Guard

Often a fencer can use the large guard of his epee to ward off attacks to the arm or hand.

Parries

It's best to use those parries that take an opponent's blade outside of your own.

Parry 6

Pretty much the same as in foil.

Parry 8

Same as foil.

Parry 2

Something new. This is a strong parry and prevents an opponent from forcing his way through. The hand position allows for a quick riposte.

Ripostes

Remember, in epee there's no right of way. Your parry won't prevent your opponent from continuing his attack because of lost priority. A riposte in opposition is your safest bet. For example, if you make a parry 6,

Parrying with the epee guard.

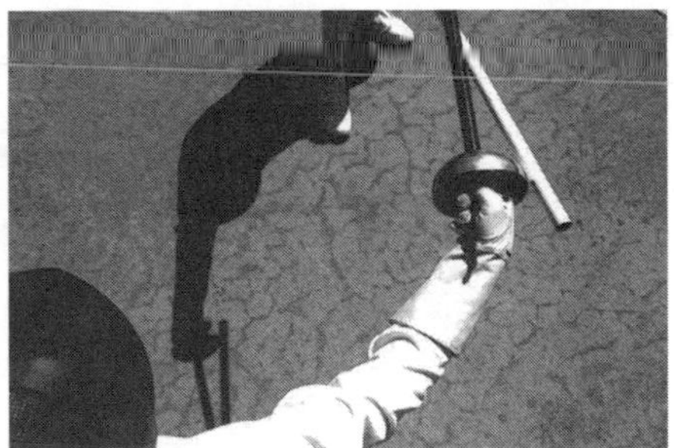

6th Position

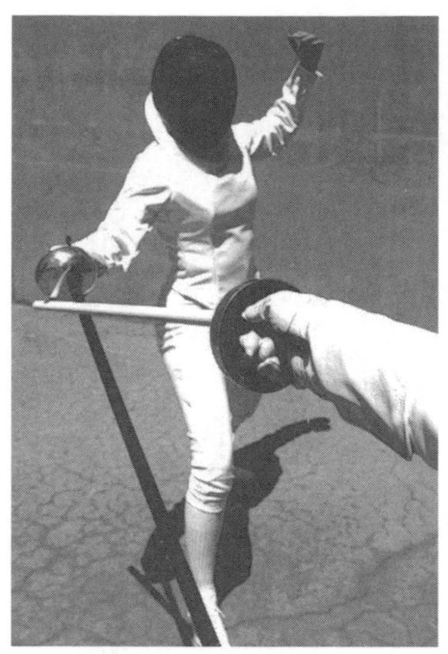

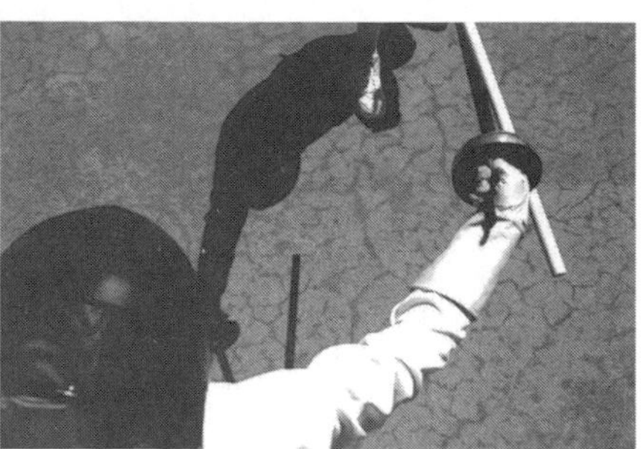

8th Position

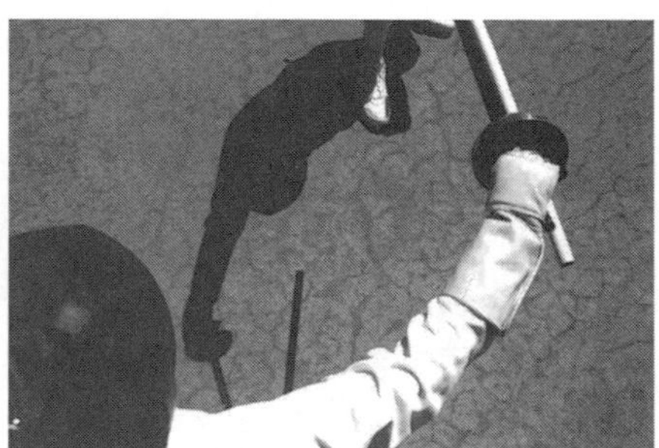

2nd Position

your opponent's blade will be on the outside of your blade. You can continue to control his blade with the forte and guard of your blade as you make the riposte.

Offense

The target area can be divided into three areas:

1. A fencer's leading foot, leg, arm and hand.
2. The torso and head.
3. The rear leg, arm and back.

Straight Thrust

Same as in foil except for those hits placed around the guard or horizontally (a target surface parallel to the floor, such as an arm or thigh). The latter requires a bit more wrist action and practice to perfect.

Disengagement

This common tactic is used to strike a number of target areas. It is often used when an opponent begins to engage blades: the fencer quickly disengages and touches the exposed arm. Again, wrist action is needed to attack around the bell of the guard.

Counter-Disengagement

This can deceive an opponent's attempt to change engagement or to make a circular parry. As his blade makes the new engagement, follow his blade around until you are clear to make the hit on his arm. A hit on the torso requires that you make this action in opposition (in such a manner that his blade is deflected harmlessly to the outside as you attack).

Compound Attacks

These actions are the same as in foil except you have a larger and more varied target. For example, you can feint to the arm and attack to the body. Your opponent may very well counter-attack into your attack instead of parrying, however, if the feint does not deceive.

Compound Ripostes

The same as compound attacks except they're preceded by successful parries. It's important that your feints draw your opponent's blade before you commit because an epeeist's usual trick after an attack is a remise, or a continuation of the attack.

Counter-Attacks

As there is no right of way, a favorite tactic of epeeists is to attack into an opponent's attack. If you touch each other within 1/25 of a second, you both score. If all you need to win is one point and your opponent needs two or more, then a double hit is all you need. If the attack is made at your torso, a stop hit to the weapon hand or arm may earn you a touch before he can hit you within the split second margin.

Stop Hits

A stop hit in opposition, where your blade is simultaneously deflecting your opponent's point while finding it's target, is, again, the safest way to make the action.

Takings of the Blade *(Prises de Fer)*

Attacks in Opposition

These start the same as attacks in foil but finish with the attacker's blade pushing through the opponent's blade, deflecting it out of line while maintaining contact and domination.

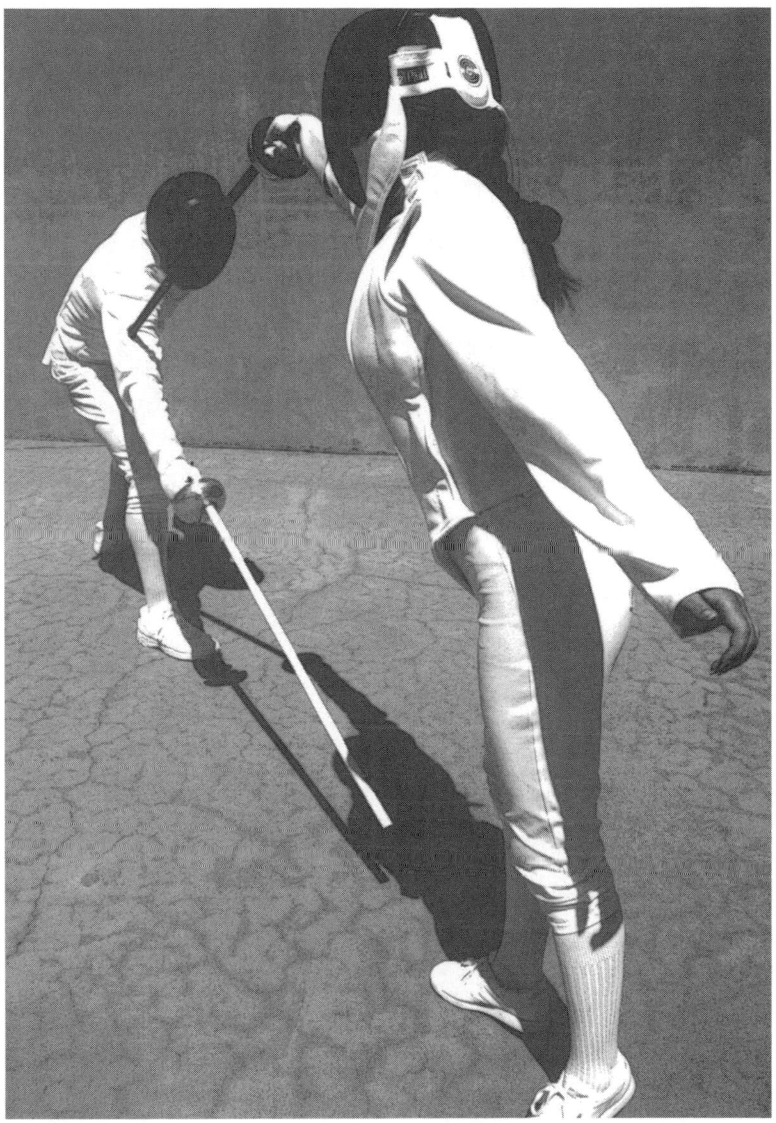

Ole! A ***stop hit*** in epee can look very much like a bull-fighter's move.

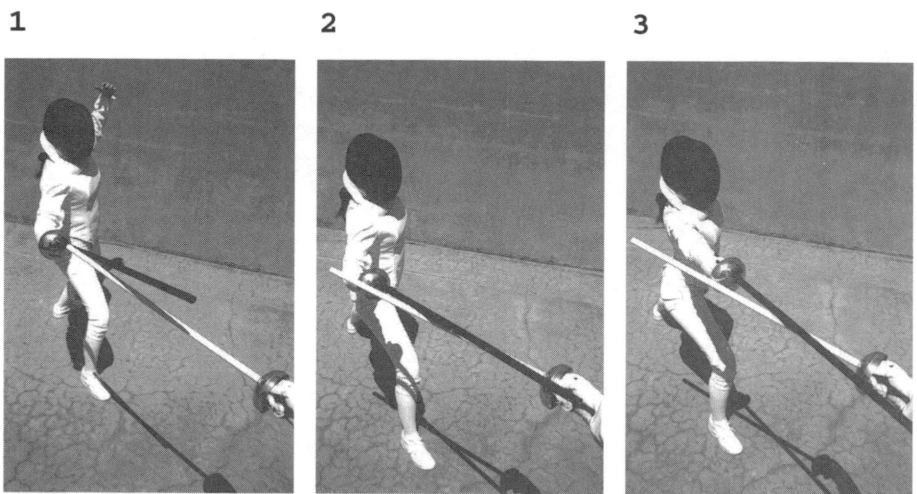

Attack in Opposition: As Olivia pushes her attack forward, her blade holds dominance over Nestor's and deflects his blade out of line.

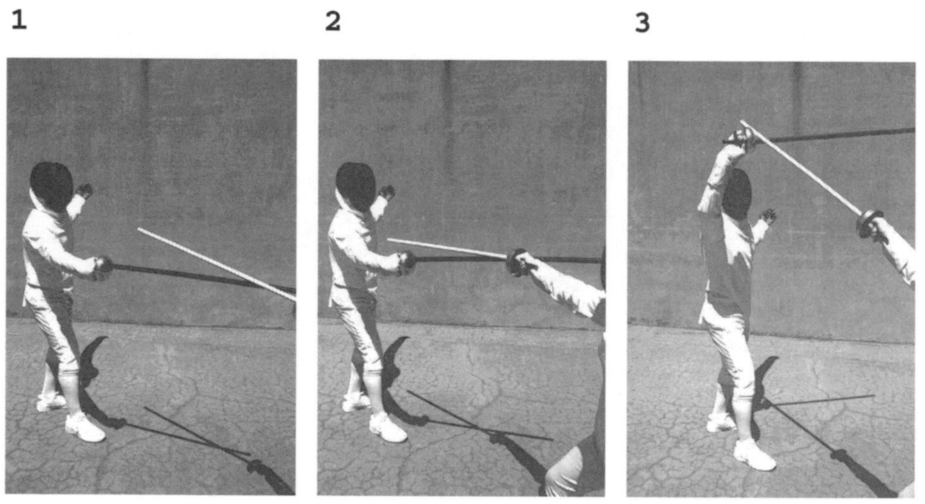

Ceding Parry: Olivia's attack in opposition is nearly complete when Nestor lifts the handle of his weapon and takes her blade out of line.

Defense Against Takings of the Blade

Opposition Parry
This is a parry of the final action of a prise de fer.

Ceding Parry
In this action your blade "takes" the attacking blade while you lift your weapon hand. Guide the blade into another line.

Renewals of Attack

In epee, it's safer to continue the offensive if parried.

Remise (rem-ees): A renewal in the same line.

Redoublement: A renewal in the lunge position.

Reprise (re-pre-z): A renewal after first recovering to on guard.

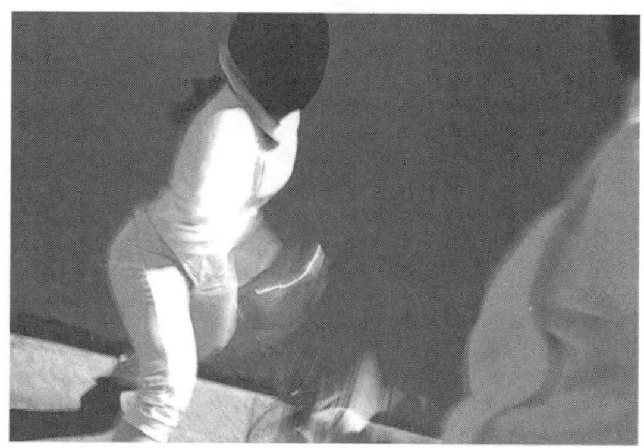

Saber = Flash!

Chapter Nine:

Charge! Saber

The fencing saber is the sleek descendent of the cavalry sword. Since you can score by cutting as well as thrusting, saber fencing has larger, more dramatic movements than foil or epee. It's an exciting and flashing way to fence that appeals to legions of true believers. Although its swashbuckling characteristics are attractive to newcomers, it's usually advised that beginners first learn foil. Without the discipline and experience of foil, there's a tendency to merely whale away. As exciting as that may seem at first, without training and technique it gets old fast.

Saber Basics

Head Banging

It's very important to have a sturdy mask because head cuts are a big part of this sport.

The Weapon

The saber has a cutting edge as well as a point. Cuts are permitted with the entire leading edge of the blade and the upper third of the backside. Although you can score by thrusting, cutting accounts for most of the scoring in saber. The guard is large and wraps around the hand, unlike the foil or epee.

New Target Area

The target is everything above the waist. Like epee, there is a forward target. The sword hand and arm are vulnerable to attack.

Right of Way

Like foil, there is a right of way rule, or convention, in saber fencing. Priority is given to the first fencer who straightens his arm and continuously threatens the target with the point or cutting edge of his weapon.

New Grip

The saber is held in a more perpendicular manner than the foil. The thumb rests on top of the handle opposite the cutting edge of the blade. The handle rests on the first knuckle of the index finger. There is a gap between the base of the thumb and the handle. The other fingers wrap around the grip and provide support. Like a golfer's grip on his club, the handle is held in the fingers and not the palm.

On Guard

Similar to on guard in foil. However, care must be taken to protect both arms as they are targets in saber. Placing the rear hand on your back hip is a good habit, although it may be necessary to remove it occasionally

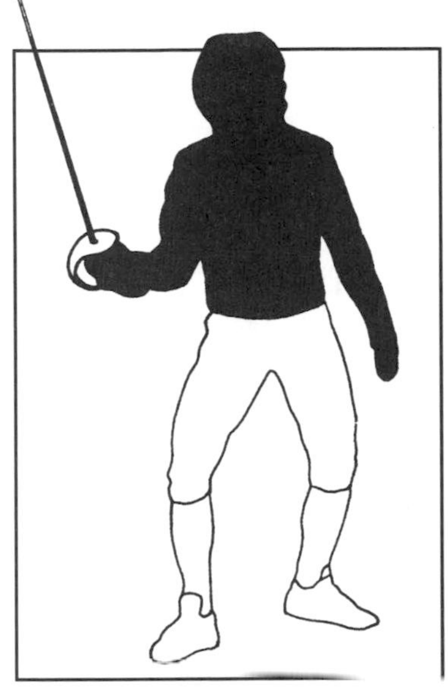

Saber Target

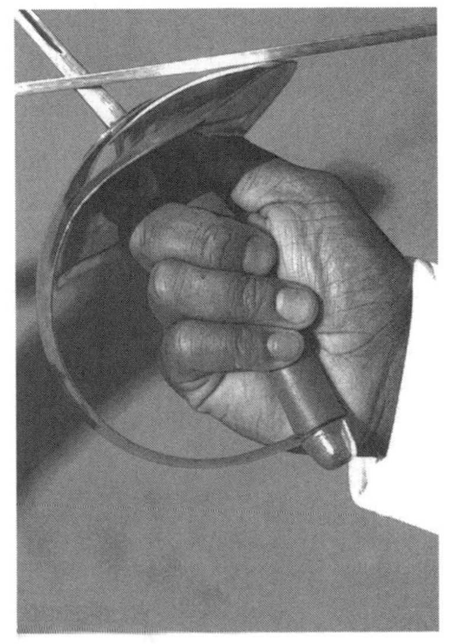

Saber Grip

On Guard

Saber fencers in ***on guard.***

Extending the arm and showing ***right of way.***

Making the cut.

to maintain proper balance. The sword arm holds the weapon with the cutting edge and guard facing your opponent. The hand is held slightly below the elbow. The forearm is parallel to the floor. The elbow is held close to the forward hip. The blade is held at a 45 degree angle.

Footwork

Same as foil except the stance is more erect and the lunge a little shorter.

Fencing Distance

Fencing distance is the same as epee. In both epee and saber, a fencer must judge distance from the sword arm, which is the closest target.

Making the Hit

Cuts

The cutting action in fencing is not a whack with a flailing arm. Cuts are made by placing the blade on the target and flexing the blade with the wrist and fingers. The cut is delivered with a forward motion, not a pulling, or drawing, motion.

Through Cut

Is made with a circular action of the wrist. The blade is pulled back into on guard.

Thrust Touches

These are like the point touches made with a foil, except that the thrust is made with the knuckles up so the blade bends properly.

Defense

Parries Against the Thrust

Thrusting attacks are parried as they are in foil.

Parries Against the Cut

To defend against cutting attacks, there are three basic parries:

Parry 3

We've already covered this. This is the on guard position. The elbow is pulled in. The hand is to the right and held lower than the elbow. The thumb is at nine o'clock. The blade is held at a 45 degree angle and protects the outside line. The guard is aimed at the opponent in order to protect the sword arm.

Parry 4

Similar to foil parry 4 and protects the inside line.

Parry 5

Held above the head and protects your noggin.

In all three parries, the cutting edge parries the attacking blade.

3rd Position

4th Position

5th Position

Note that in all positions, Olivia parries with the cutting edge of her saber.

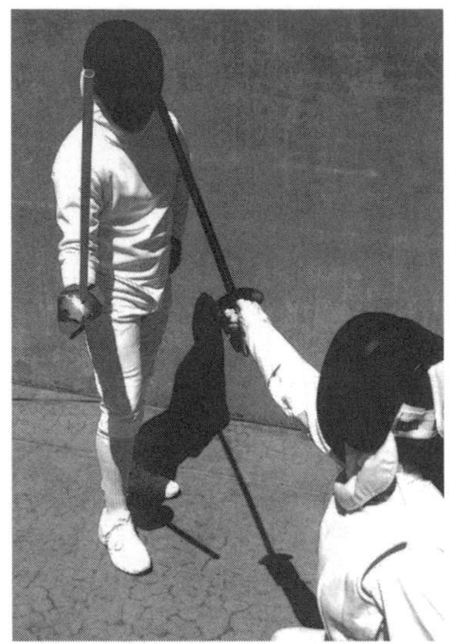

Head cut

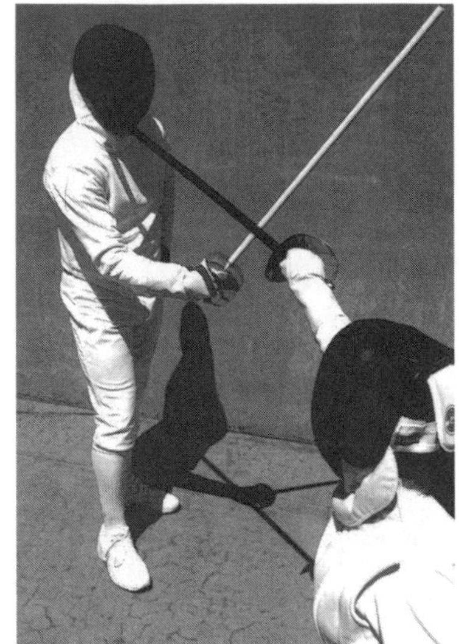

Cheek cut

Flank cut

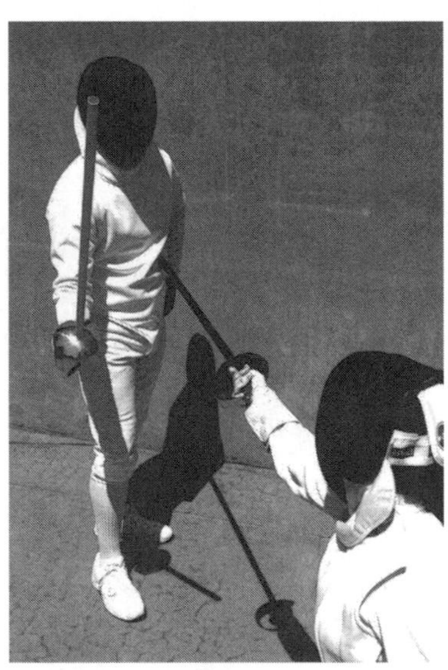

Belly or chest cut

Offense

Targets and hand positions:

Head Cut

The saber arrives at the head with the thumb of the sword hand at twelve o'clock. Slice forward.

Flank Cut

The saber is held knuckles up and slices forward.

Left Cheek Cut

Held knuckles up, the saber slices forward.

Right Cheek Cut

Held knuckles down, the saber slices forward.

Chest or Belly Cut

The saber is held knuckles down and is pulled or drawn to make the cut.

Cuts to an opponent's wrist and arm are more difficult to make and take some time to develop. They're also risky because such cuts usually expose the attacker's sword arm.

Point Thrusts

Can be very effective because they are unexpected. They are difficult to parry because it takes a change of gears to switch from the sweeping motions of the parries that defend against the cuts to the tighter parries that are effective against the thrust.

Compound Attacks

Can be quite varied. A saber fencer can use both thrusting and cutting attacks on any number of target areas.

Saber Overview

Saber and foil tactics are similar since both are governed by the convention of right of way. The differences stem from the two methods of attack allowed in saber (cutting with an edge and thrusting with a point) and the larger target area.

Distance is critical. The sword arm is a forward target and often vulnerable. You must learn to vary your distance constantly and to keep your sword arm protected. Sword movements must be tight and controlled. Wide swings will expose the sword arm to attacks.

Most attacks in saber are made with cuts rather than thrusts. Cuts come in at an angle and defending them is very difficult. As a result, fencers try to avoid the blade on the attack and try to find it when defending.

Defenders also use second intention defensive actions to pinpoint their opponent's target. A second intention is a planned action after a feint or invitation. In other words, through a convincing bluff, you create the target for your opponent. Since you know where he's gonna attack, you know where to defend.

It's clever to mix the point attack with the cut because saber fencers, in general, often forget about the thrust.

The ***point thrust*** is used sparingly in saber. It may, however, catch your opponent by surprise and be particularly useful if his parries aren't good against the thrust ...

... but the point attack entails extending the arm, thus cxposing it to an arm or wrist cut.

Their are numerous ways to make the ***compound attack:***

From on guard ...

... Olivia feints a chest cut (below) and makes an arm cut.

In the next two pix she feints to the head and cuts the flank.

Here she feints to Nestor's chest and cuts his head.

Olivia takes Nestor's blade into a ***bind*** in the following five pix. Note that Nestor's arm is extended and Olivia is using her forte on his foible. Both of those things have to happen in order for the bind to work.

1

2

3

4

5

Olivia makes the ***stop hit*** on Nestor's wrist using the back of her blade (the upper third of the blade's back is a cutting edge).

Some Saber Tips

Offensively, look for:

- Your opponent's exposed sword arm.
- His ability to parry thrust attacks.
- A head that leans too far forward.

Defensively, remember to:

- Parry with the cutting edge.
- Return to on guard immediately after the attack.
- Back up when you parry.

An ***exposed sword arm*** gets severed ...

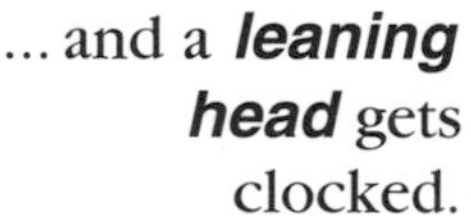

... and a ***leaning head*** gets clocked.

Chapter Ten

FunStuff
Sport Fencing

Evolution/Revolution

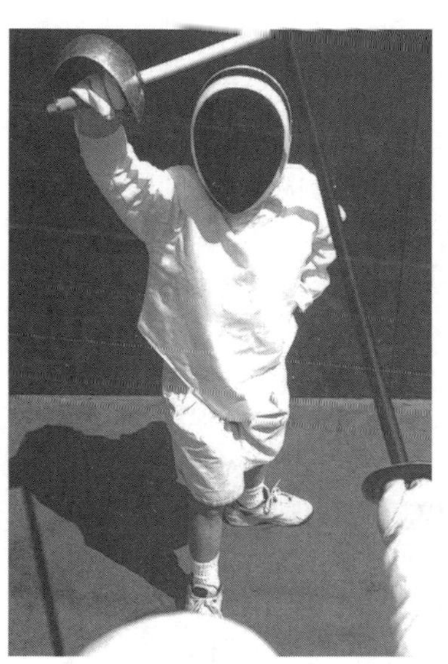

Fencing is hardly the high-toned, insular pursuit it used to be. A new awareness from within and without has influenced the modern game and broadened its appeal. As fencing charges into yet another century, it finds itself on the cutting edge of dynamic leisure activity.

Sport Fencing, a new form of recreational fencing, is especially well suited for today's active sportsperson. It provides hot action, a torrid workout and unfettered fun. It's an exciting way to get started with this fencing business.

Check it out ...

Unplugged

No wires. Natural. Sport Fencing is a simplified, non-electrical form of fencing that enables fencers to bout outside(!) of the studio. It can be played on any flat, nonskid surface. Patios, tennis courts, basketball courts and airport runways are excellent surfaces upon which to play.

Saber Flavored

Sport Fencing utilizes the saber as its basic weapon and much of the technique is based on Olympic-style saber fencing. The crashing blades and fast action of saber are perfectly suited to the fun and spirit of Sport Fencing, which for all intents and purposes is a true action sport (*i.e.*, a hip, aerobically supercharged thrill trip).

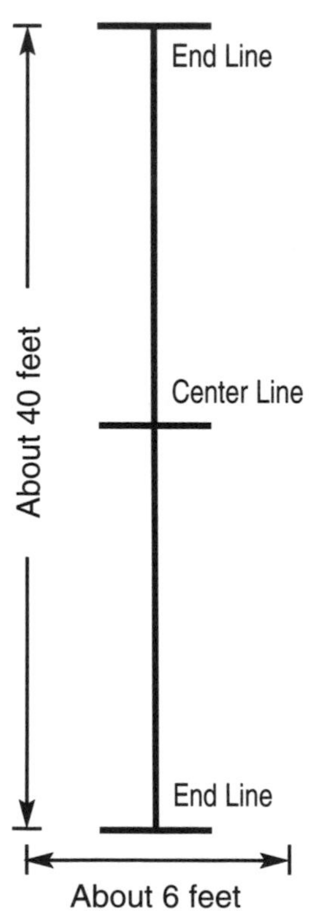

All Ya Need Is Chalk

Like Olympic-style fencing, action is linear (straight up and back). Fencers face off along a chalk line about 40 feet in length and must stay within 3 feet of it at all times. Play is stopped whenever the players find themselves at the end of the line or too far away from it. So much for a complicated playing field.

The idea, of course, is to hit or touch your opponent with the tip or edge of your saber. The valid target area is anything above the waist.

Got all that?

Geared up! With mask, glove and jacket secure and fitted, Griffin is ready to cross blades. Note the distinctive guard of the saber.

Central to Sport Fencing is ***right of way***. Here Griffin gains right of way by extending his saber and making a threat.

If the other guy attacks first, you have to block or parry his blade in order to gain priority or right of way.

Playing the Game

Players must first gain right of way before their hits are valid. Fencers gain priority by extending the saber at their opponents and initiating an attack or by blocking an attack and initiating their own counter-attack. The concept of right of way eliminates mindless thrashing (it does get old) and adds some cerebral dimension (madly exuberant foreplay) to the game.

Scoring is optional (if you just gotta win, try Olympic-style fencing or coach Little League). The idea here is to get some exercise, make the smooth move and have fun. If you're gonna score it's sorta like tennis. Players fence up to five bouts. Three out of five wins. The winner of each bout is the first to score seven hits or touches.

Players line up at the center of the chalk line with about 10 feet of separation. One fencer asks "*Fencers ready?*" and the other replies "*Ready!*" when he's indeed ready, and the bout begins. Action continues up and back along the chalk line until a touch is made or someone goes out of bounds. When either occurs, play is halted and the fencers start over as before.

Stuff to keep in mind as you begin to play includes the distance you keep between yourself and your opponent. You want to be far enough away to successfully avoid attack, but close enough to score yourself. Wise use of fencing distance is absolutely key in this sport.

Instruction and practice drills pay off in fencing. Books help (even this one), but nothing replaces a good coach, helpful classmates and drilling the maneuvers until they become second nature.

All You Need to Know

The beauty of Sport Fencing is its simplicity. Here are the basics in plain English.

Grip

Like golf, fundamentals start with the grip. And like golf, the handle is held with the fingers and not the palm. The thumb rests on top, opposite the cutting edge. There's a bit of space between the base of the thumb and the handle.

On Guard

On guard is the ready position. Stance is shoulder-width or so with the knees slightly bent. Torso is erect and sideways to your opponent to minimize the target area. The front foot points toward your target at all times, and the rear foot is positioned at a right angle to the target line. The sword arm is three quarters extended and is held to the side to protect the outside line. The cutting edge is directed at your opponent with the point of the blade about chest high. The other arm serves as a counterbalance and is held up behind the torso or with the hand resting on the rear hip.

Right of Way

You must remember right of way! He who initiates the attack first may try to score. The other guy must first block or parry the attack in order to attack himself. This attack/parry/counter-attack can become an extended affair, much like a rally in tennis. This give and take is an essential part of Sport Fencing and is called phrasing. It's also what makes this stuff fun. And a heckuva workout!

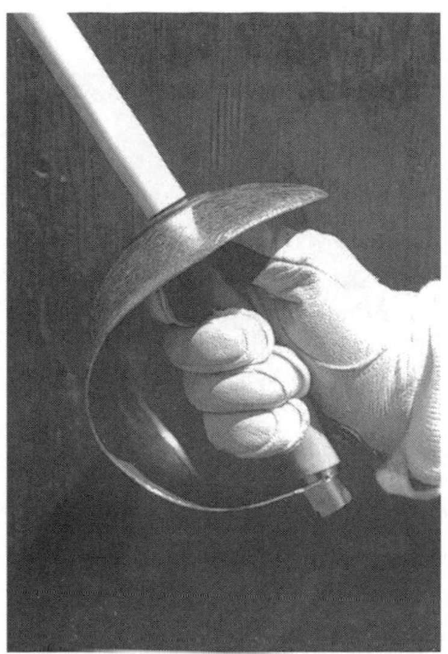

Grip: The thumb lines up on the opposite side of the cutting edge of the saber. Grip is firm, not tight.

On guard: Griffin is ready to move up or back in perfect combat trim. His sword arm is 3/4 extended. Since his hand is a target, he keeps it rested on his back hip.

1 2 3

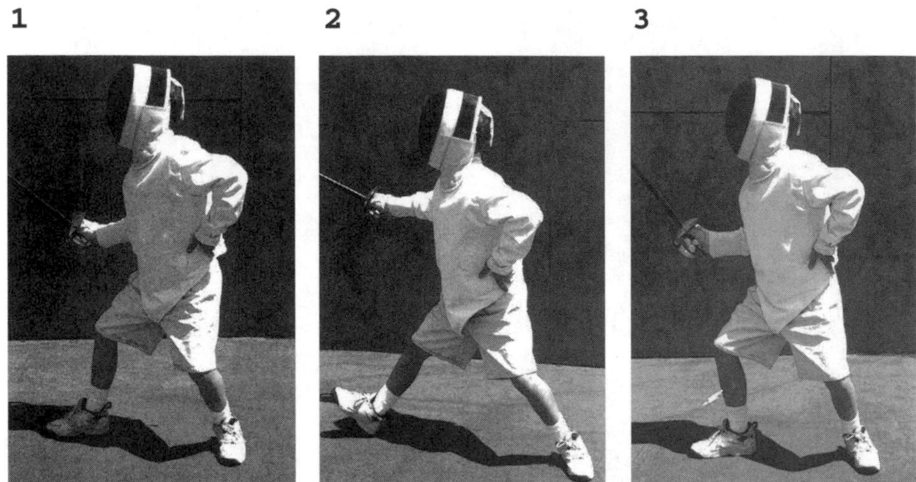

Advancing: Pushing off his back foot, Griffin steps forward in smooth staccato steps.

1 2 3

Retreating: Pushing off his front foot this time, Griffin demonstrates an important part of his defensive game – keeping his fencing distance!

Advancing and Retreating

Moving around and adjusting the fencing distance is an important part of the game. A fencer will close the distance to orchestrate an attack, and he will open the distance to defend himself. To move forward from the on guard position, push off the rear foot and advance the front foot a comfortable distance, keeping your toes pointed forward. Then bring the rear foot up an equal distance so that your feet are once again in the original on guard position. Keep the distance between your feet constant whenever you move! To retreat, push off the front foot first and place the rear foot back a comfortable distance, keeping the right angle of the foot intact throughout. Then take the front foot back an equal distance so that your feet are once again in the original on guard position.

These movements are most successful when feet j-u-s-t skim the surface and bouncing is held to a minimum. Smooth is the word.

Thrust

This is an extension of the sword arm with the point of the blade directed at your opponent. All attacks must include this action.

Lunge and Recovery

The most common way to deliver a touch is with a lunge. This is a rapid forward movement executed first by extending the sword arm, followed by a large forward stride propelled by the extension of the rear leg. To recover from the lunge, either step back with the front leg or bring the rear leg forward into the on guard position.

Attack Actions

A simple attack involves a single blade action. A compound attack is a series of blade actions linked together in order to orchestrate an offensive designed to "get ahead" of an opponent. For example, a fencer may fake an attack (the first blade action) in order to draw a particular response that he can deceive with another blade action (the second blade action) and make a touch. So "getting ahead" means keeping your opponent busy with defensive actions as you weave your attack.

It's important to remember that all blade actions are accompanied by footwork. The advance, thrust and lunge will close the distance between you and your opponent so you may successfully utilize your weapon. By the way, there are no running attacks allowed in Sport Fencing (a little too dangerous).

Blade Actions

Contact: When blades come into contact.

Disconnect: With the fencing arm fully extended, the point of the weapon is moved from one side of the opponent's blade to the other. This action is generally followed by an attack.

Thrust: As previously discussed, the rapid extension of the fencing arm and weapon. The saber is held palm up while the point is directed at the target.

Beat: A quick tap to an opponent's blade in order to surprise, deflect his point out of line or initiate a counter-attack.

1

2

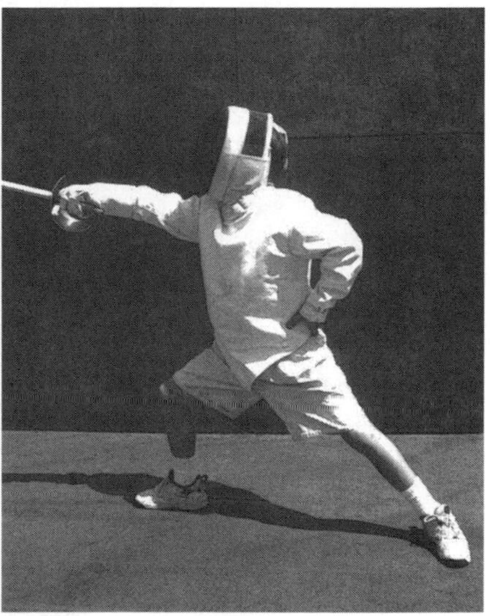

Lunge and recovery

3

The lunge is the final action in 99 percent of your offensive moves. From on guard Griffin extends his sword arm and makes a power push off his rear foot. Note his rear leg is straight and his back foot stays flat. He recovers by bringing his back foot up into on guard.

Beat attack: Griffin scores by slapping his Dad's blade off target and lunging with a straight thrust.

Scoring with a ***head cut.*** This is a very common way to score in Sport Fencing as the head is often a forward target and left unprotected.

Arm/wrist cut: Fencers often score with a cut on an opponent's exposed sword arm. This illustrates the importance of protecting the arm behind the guard of your blade as well as maintaining your fencing distance.

Bind: Taking an opponent's blade from a high-line position on one side to the opposite low-line position.

Glide: Gliding the blade forward on an opponent's blade.

Coupe (koo-pay)***:*** A quick cutting motion over an opponent's blade. Generally followed by a lunge and a cutting motion with the wrist.

Cruise: Taking an opponent's blade from a high-line position to the low-line position on the same side.

Dig: A sharp, single blade action and attack to an opponent's forearm.

Orbit: Taking an opponent's blade in a circular motion without release followed by an attack into the open line.

Fake: A blade action intended to draw a reaction from an opponent. Usually followed by at least one more blade action.

Dare: A deliberate act intended to tempt an opponent to attack.

Press: Putting pressure on an opponent's blade in order to draw a response.

Remo: A quick replacement of the point on target after an initial attack. The fencing arm has remained extended throughout.

Defensive Actions

The parry and the retreat are the two forms of defense in Sport Fencing.

The parry is a blade movement that deflects an opponent's attacking blade. It also establishes right of way, as described earlier, so that a fencer may initiate a counter-attack.

The retreat opens the distance between fencers and enables a fencer to avoid blade action and to increase reaction time.

In Sport Fencing we use a simple, triangulated defensive technique. As noted in the photograph, this defense has two facets. The "head" parry defends the head and the two "flank" parries defend the flanks.

Another important and useful defensive technique is the yielding parry. This parry is used against attacks involving takings of the blade, which are offensive blade actions that dominate and control an opponent's blade during an attack or counter-attack. To execute, the defender must keep his arm fully extended and offer no opposition throughout the attack until the last moment. As the attacking blade moves in for the touch, the defender then lifts his handle and moves the attacking blade into another line. It's important to keep blade contact throughout this action. Patience and timing are critical.

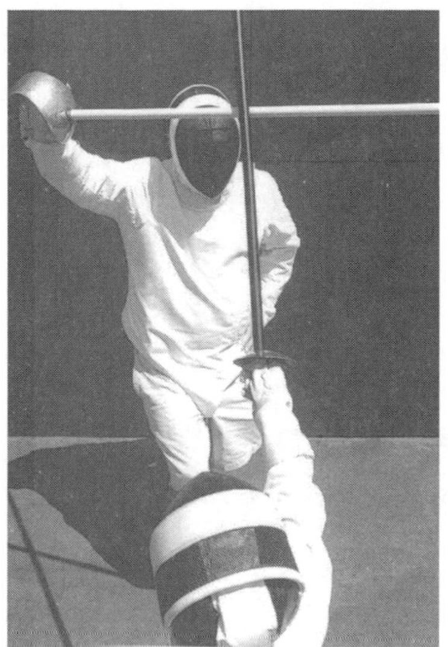

Head parry

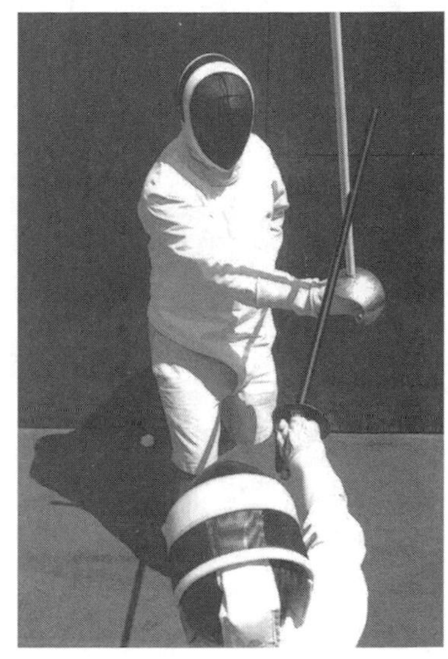

Flank parries

Defending with the saber: The word "fence" comes from "defense," and Chris Reinhard shows how it's done Sport Fencer's style.These three parries are all you need to ward off attack.

From on guard, Chris makes a threat ...

... that Griffin parries in order to make his own threat ...

... that Chris parries in order to make his own threat ...

... that Griffin parries in order to make the score.

The Spirit of Sport Fencing

A spirited, fun and controlled competition is always encouraged. Efficient, economical and creative fencing technique combined with extended engagements for aerobic exercise are where it's at. Simply scoring a touch is not the object of Sport Fencing. Keeping score is not all that important. If raw competition is your game, try Olympic-style fencing.

Combative behavior is out. There's absolutely no body contact allowed. And no running attacks. Sport Fencing is intended to build friendship and trust. It's about having good, clean fun with your fellow fencer. Psychos, bullies and blowhards need not apply.

A conversation between blades: What's really cool is the extended "rally" or exchange that can happen between fencers.

Sport Fencing Glossary

Comparable to the traditional fencer's glossary, but this one you can read, pronounce and understand.

Advance: Stepping forward while maintaining on guard.

Attack: An offensive action that seeks to register a scoring touch on an opponent.

Ballsout: A fast and continuous jumping lunge. Also known as a balestra.

Beat: A quick tap to an opponent's blade in order to surprise, deflect an opponent's point out of line or to initiate a counter-attack.

Bind: Taking an opponent's blade on a diagonal from a high-line position to a low-line position on the opposite side.

Changing the Line: Moving the blade over or under an opponent's blade from the right to the left.

Connect: Blades crossed and in contact. Also known as an engagement.

Counter-Attack: A fencer's offensive action after successfully parrying an opponent's attack.

Coupe (koo-pay)***:*** A quick cutting motion over an opponent's blade. Generally followed by a lunge and a cutting motion with the wrist.

Cruise: Taking an opponent's blade from a high-line position to the corresponding low-line. Also known as a croise.

Dare: A deliberate act intended to tempt an opponent to attack. Also known as an invitation.

Derobe: A blade movement made to avoid contact with an opponent's attack on the blade. Also known as a derobement.

Defense: An action that seeks to stop or neutralize an opponent's offensive action.

Dig: A sharp, single blade action and attack to an opponent's forearm.

Disconnect: With the fencing arm fully extended, the point of the weapon is moved from one side of the opponent's blade to the other. This action is generally followed by an attack. Also known as a disengagement.

Explosion: A strong motion with the wrist and forearm followed by a straight thrust. This action may disarm an opponent. Also known as an expulsion.

Fake: A blade action intended to draw a reaction from an opponent. Usually followed by at least one more blade action. Also known as a feint.

Getting Ahead: A series of planned and well-executed offensive actions that keep an opponent on the defensive. Should result in a touch.

Glide: A light sliding action on an opponent's blade intended to draw a parry and create an opening for an attack.

Orbit: Taking an opponent's blade in a sweeping, circular motion without release. This action is followed by an attack into the open line. Also known as an envelopment.

Parry: A defensive blade action that prevents an opponent's blade from arriving on target.

Patio: A very rapid and continuous lunge. Also known as an advance lunge.

Press: Putting pressure on an opponent's blade in order to draw a response.

Ready Position: An equilibrium state that allows a fencer to be ready to attack or defend at any moment during a fencing bout. Also known as on guard.

Redo: The renewal of an attack while still in the lunge position. Also known as a redoublement.

Remo: A quick replacement of the point on target after an initial attack. The fencing arm remains extended throughout. Also known as a remise.

Retreat: Stepping back while maintaining on guard.

Rip: A counter-attack made immediately after a parry.

Thrust: The rapid extension of the fencing arm and

weapon. The saber is held palm up while the point is directed at the target.

Touch: A clear hit to an opponent's target area once a fencer has established right of way.

This guy throws steel because he thinks it's cool.

Any arguments?

Sport Fencing Equipment and Gear

There's some stuff you'll need: the Winsor Sport saber, protective glove, mask, jacket and pants for sure. You'll also need athletic shoes designed for basketball, tennis or racquetball. Men should wear a cup and women should wear chest protection. Always wear protective gear and apparel before crossing blades!

Winsor Sport Fencing has developed a complete line of ultrahip, quality Sport Fencing gear and sportswear.

www.winsorsport.com

A Beginner's Journal

Five Months & Forty-Seven Lessons

(Warning!)

This journal is the day-by-day history of my initial involvement with fencing. I had my first lesson at the beginning of one November and my 47th(!) by the following March. I'm still going but enough's enough.

That's five months, man! I've never spent five months learning anything in my life. But unlike higher education, it was fun 95 percent of the time, and thanks to the program and the coach, 100 percent worthwhile. It really is a fine pursuit, this fencing.

The journal is a bit long, but I don't know where to cut it (yet) so here it is. Like any journal, it's good for background and there are nuggets of knowledge to be shared. But the best parts are the funny parts.

Read at least the first 20 pages or so because it'll give you blank-slaters a good idea of what it's like to start. The story about me rumbling with a ferocious 12-year-old is about as entertaining as I can get. So if it's a drag at that point, forget it.

Doug Werner

11-1: What the Heck

I know that fencers wear white outfits and masks. They sorta prance about and hold themselves like ballet dancers. It's a sport steeped in tradition, custom and romance. The swordplay looks like fun, but not the bouting ritual. Too many rules or something. It seems to me that it would be a whole lot cooler if fencers just whacked away at each other like they do in the movies, but what do I know. It strikes me as an elitist endeavor forever doomed to be enjoyed by a few college students, their professors and the idle rich.

It strikes me as an elitist endeavor forever doomed to be enjoyed by a few college students, their professors and the idle rich.

But what the heck. It's *different*. And a friend who knows says it's great stuff. Besides, playing swords was fun when I was a kid. So I find a school in the Yellow Pages, discover that lessons are fairly cheap and show up the next day in sweats and sneakers.

11-2: First Day

The studio is located in an iffy part of town. Just a storefront with lots of space. Everything is a little beat up. There's marks on the floor for something, wires hanging from the ceiling and lots of pictures on the walls. Nothing intimidating here. Scruffy and definitely not stuffy.

The master or instructor or whatever is Jack. He's the only one there and has me fill out a couple of forms. Then he suits me up in mask, glove and tunic. The mask pops over my head, the padded glove protects my sword hand (my right hand) and the tunic is a canvas material that covers torso, arms and groin with straps that travel between the legs and attach in back. Everything fits OK and I feel pretty comfy. He helps me pick out a sword (foil) from the rack and I'm ready-freddy.

The rest of the class includes a younger fellow and his girlfriend. Like me, they picked the place out of the phone book and signed

I get sweaty and start to think I'm an actor in a Richard Simmons workout video.

up on a lark. A more advanced bunch also shows and they're an endearing mix of little ones and teenagers.

Jack leads our tiny group off to one side. He's the only instructor and over the course of the hour-long lesson he bounces back and forth between the two groups. We start out by doing a series of stretching exercises. I know this is an important thing to do before any physical endeavor, but stretching has always been a big bore for me. When I'm ready to play I wanna play. It's like going to an awards function hungry. Who wants to listen to speeches before they serve the food?

He has my group assume a peculiar foot position that looks and feels a lot like some sort of dance pose. The foot we each choose to be the lead foot is pointed straight ahead at an imaginary target and the other is drawn behind it at a right angle. We are then told to make the distance between our feet about shoulder width. Knees are flexed. Shoulders must align with the target line indicated by the lead foot. Arms are held up. The sword hand and arm point ahead along the target line and the rear arm is bent at the elbow with the thumb pointing at the back of the head. Since we are standing in front of a wall of mirrors, we can check ourselves out.

Getting it right is easy to do. It's just a matter of copying the universal image we all have of the swordsman ready to cross swords. This, of course, is the on guard position. There's nothing else like it except maybe in ballet. The distinct positioning of feet, bent legs and balanced arms is imprinted on my mind before I even try.

Moving around is a little more tricky. Jack teaches us to lift the front foot slightly and to push off the instep to propel forward, and to lift the rear foot slightly and to push off the toes of the front foot to move backward. Moving is strictly a forward and backward thing. No turning or circles. The idea is to maintain the shoulder-width stance, the flexed knees and the right-angled feet as you scoot straight up and straight back. It's funky, awkward and my first indication that fencing ain't a snap.

Jack says to practice while he engages the other group. So we three scoot and shuffle and hop in front of the mirror. What looked like a dance step *is* a dance step and getting it right is just as difficult to learn. It takes technique, coordination, rhythm and muscles that have never been used. I get sweaty and start to think I'm an actor in a Richard Simmons workout video.

We kinda get that down but Jack comes back with some curve balls. He shows us some *stepping* maneuvers to work into the *scooting* maneuvers and tells us to mix it up. Right. Now it's really like Arthur Murray because mixing it up requires a dancer's memory that I simply don't have. Not that the stepping maneuvers are difficult (it's really just stepping). But it's befuddling to scoot and step in sync. He leaves us again and it gets ugly. It's hot in my tunic and, heck, I'm getting winded.

Jack finally returns, asks us to stop our crabbing about and to don our masks and pick up our swords. He points to a figure drawn on the chalkboard and explains that the torso is divided into quadrants. They are numbered 4, 6, 7, and 8. To defend these target zones, a fencer must learn defensive techniques. They are called parries: the parry of 4, the parry of 6, the parry of 7 and the parry of 8. Each parry has a different sword hand and arm position. The differences seem rather slight, but apparently these differences are very important. As Jack goes around and molds our hands properly in the four positions, I discover how uncomfortable these parry positions are to hold. It really seems convoluted and because we don't know how these parries really work in action, practicing these contortions seems silly.

With time running out, Jack shows us how to do an extension and a lunge. Again, the nuances of these maneuvers are dancelike and precise. Sloppiness is not in the fencing lexicon. There is an exact way to do this stuff and improv is simply out of the question.

The lunge is cool because it has a connection to swordplay (childhood memories) that the parry business doesn't. It's a lively straight ahead plunge with the sword propelled by the back foot. We practice with dummies and Jack shows us how to stab with the point so that the blade bends up and not down.

> **He says not to worry: that everything about fencing is natural. But that I will feel like a duck in the beginning.**

We beginners take a break and watch the other students cross swords. It's a pretty complicated business. Each student needs to hook up with a wire that plugs into the sword handle, runs up the sleeve, out the back of the tunic and extends up to the ceiling and to a buzzer. The wires are on a track that allows the fencers to travel forward and backward in a straight line. I think of cable cars as I watch two very small fencers thrash away at each other until the buzzer sounds, indicating that one of the participants has touched his opponent and thus, scored a touch.

At one point the buzzer sounds and doesn't shut off. Jack has to fiddle with the wires and the connections to find the source of the problem. After about a minute of buzzing, he discovers that one of the young fencers has unplugged his foil. The mechanism works when it works and apparently is the accepted technology, but I find it difficult to believe in this age of high gizmology that there isn't a better way to track the touches of the foil on an opponent. Good grief! If someone told me about an activity that requires people to bound around with wires wrapped around themselves, underneath a pulley contraption strung from the ceiling, I would assume that they were discussing Nazi atrocities. The technology is midcentury at best and the concept medieval. This sport is screaming for the future!

Class is dismissed after a drill or two and I ask Jack about the awkwardness of the parries. He says not to worry: that everything about fencing is natural and that it'll come together soon enough. But that I will feel like a duck in the beginning.

11-5: Lesson #2: Hi! My Name is Ivan!

Tonight there's a larger group. No kids. Ranging in age from 18 or so to 40-ish. The beginners from my first class aren't here. This group looks more advanced, but hardly major league. Everybody is friendly and loose.

Jack calls for a gathering to introduce a visiting fencing master from Russia. His name is Ivan, and he's here for a week. He'll be teaching the class tonight. Jack tells us to soak up as much wisdom as possible and disappears. It's Ivan Time.

Ivan looks like a Russian. His face is elastic and expressive. He has a very direct way of looking at us with big brown friendly eyes. He's not tall, skinny or aristocratic (like I might have expected, for some reason) and all in all, very engaging. "Hi!" he says to us and we all say hi back.

Ivan has us line up and faces us like a kindly drill sergeant. "OK we start," he begins. "Americans do this stretcha, stretcha, stretcha. But no. Russian and German and Italian do the run to get ready for fencing. So we do. Now. Run."

The class is hesitant because Ivan's handle on the language is a tad clipped (What'd he say?). But when Ivan twirls a finger and says, "OK, run!" we all begin a jog around the studio. After a lap or two he commands us to turn sideways and keep moving in a skipping motion. After that he has us run backward. Then in a squatty forward run (groans). Then in a lower squatty run (more groans). Finally, he has us run a lap and walk a lap.

I've broken a sweat and it feels really good. Much better than the stretching exercises we did the first day. But a good third of the class is already flagged. This bunch is not particularly fit or athletic. I get the impression that most of the folks are here out of curiosity and for fencing's exotic appeal. Like it's some kind of arty experience or something. I'm certain that they weren't expecting calisthenics.

But Ivan has only begun. "OK, line up," he commands in that endearing way of his. "Do fencing position." We all assume the on guard position. He has us go through a series of drills that include advances, retreats and lunges. It's clippity-clip so we all start breathing hard. I'm at a disadvantage because I have little idea of what he's asking us to do. I'm also located at the end of the line with my back to the instructor so that I'm doing all this stuff with my head cranked 180 degrees.

I'm drenched in sweat and a little concerned that some pansy-assed fencing class has broken me down so completely.

"Breathe through your nose not your mouth," he commands (although this makes little sense to me). I steal a glance at my classmates and note that some are ready to collapse. It's obvious that old Ivan is used to a higher level of class participation and response. The flopping and grunting of our little F Troop is probably very disappointing to him, although he wears a congenial expression and hasn't yet burst into a Cassock rage. He looks my way every now and then and I see a flicker of dissatisfaction and disbelief in his eyes. Nuts! I'm screwing up in front of the master!

Undeterred, he springs the most heartless physical exercise I've ever seen upon our panting group. "Now do this," he says and from the on guard position he picks up his lead foot and balances on one foot. Then he kicks out with the suspended leg in perfect little thrusts that would shame a ballerina. Or a world-class kick boxer. This I can't do and from the thudding sounds of bodies landing around me, I gather that nobody else can either.

The class is totally worked at this point, but Ivan says it's time to put on our gear and engage. I'm drenched in sweat and a little concerned that some pansy-assed fencing class has broken me down so completely. Some among us are quietly whimpering and eyeing the clock on the wall, counting the minutes that are left in this fencing hell.

Ivan has us pair off to run through a variety of drills that I have never even heard of. Heck, I barely know how to hold the foil. A lady in the class tells the Russian that the guy back there (me) is only one lesson old. Ivan takes off his mask and comes over. "Hi, my name is Ivan," he says and smiles. "What's your name?"

"Hi, my name is Doug," I reply.

"It's OK, Doug. You try."

Sure, I say and away we go. I'm paired with Ivan who firmly explains and demonstrates everything to me as we go through the various drills. We stumble through touches and lunges and parries. There's a certain way to hold the foil, to carry your elbow, to point the tip, to place the feet, to flex the knees and to extend your arms. After awhile it becomes very tiring. Mentally and physically. It's hard to remember everything and all the muscle groups required in fencing are out of shape and out of use. My hand throbs because you maneuver the foil with only your thumb and forefinger. My arms ache because your arms are always held up and out. My legs are stiff because the on guard position requires that you turn and place your feet in a rigidly square manner.

Yet, I'm impressed and grateful that the gentleman is taking the time with me. Although he's adamant about technique and makes me correct things constantly, I realize that he's simply being a teacher and I don't feel picked upon. Despite his focus on me, he doesn't lose track of the rest of the class and when he sees something to correct in another's performance, he promptly applies the same concern for proper execution.

After a bit I pair off with another student and we go through some drills. As this student is more experienced, I follow his lead and he's kind enough to coach me through the morass of maneuvers that Ivan asks of us.

We finish with some more exercises, sans equipment. As the clock strikes eight, he has us gather around for what I assume will be some pep talk, fencer style. Instead he says, "When you get home take hot, hot shower, OK? Or bath OK, too. But very, very hot. You all work tonight very hard so tomorrow you ache. OK, good night."

11-7: Lesson #3: Not Fun

The class begins on time. We get right into the parries and I think I finally get it. I note that Ivan cuts down on the calisthenics and the lesson has a bit more structure to it. Maybe he just feels more comfortable.

Things are OK until the more complex fencing drills begin. It's

This sport is heavy on technique and nuance. It's just too darn difficult to learn from someone who has such weak command of the language.

possible to understand Ivan explain the simple things, but as soon as he tries to draw the connections between one maneuver and the next, the bottom falls out. This sport is heavy on technique and nuance. It's just too darn difficult to learn from someone who has such weak command of the language. Here's a sampling:

"You know engash? Yes? You do this. OK, now you try. Do tosh and lunge one guy, you step back parry 4, engash, show tosh and lunge. Ready?"

Ivan says something like this and the class simply stands there dumbfounded. Then, out of some sort of impulse to please (I guess) we each face our drilling partner and run through the motions, trying to figure out on our own what to do. After awhile, Ivan jumps in and shows us what he means by demonstrating or by physically pushing and pulling our bodies and body parts this way and that. It's endearing in a way and his desire to teach us is obvious, but this stuff is hard enough to learn without the communication gap. Heck, this is my third lesson and I'm still not sure if I'm holding the foil correctly.

The final breakdown occurs during a drill where one fencer advances and retreats while the other fencer tries to follow his lead in order to maintain the original distance. It starts out well enough, but after awhile my partner starts to whale away. I laugh and follow suit, but after a bit it becomes tiresome because we simply don't know what we're doing. There's no point and therefore no progress. Ivan doesn't say anything and I finally stop, take off my superheated mask and walk away. Another guy takes my place and Ivan comes over to say, "OK. You take break."

Ivan takes this opportunity to drill me through the parry positions. What I thought I knew is apparently all wrong. He tries to explain, but like earlier he ends up grabbing my wrists and placing them in position himself.

He gathers us for one more class drill and in between final exercises he mentions something about once being 270 pounds. That fencing brought his weight down to 170 and that fencing can do wonders for us all. Oh, boy. Watch out Jenny Craig.

I'm tired, slightly disgusted and when he finally says, "OK class, good night," I bolt for the door. As the cold night air hits my sweaty face, I hear the class applaud (applaud?) our Russian Master. I guess I'm the only one who feels the train has jumped the track.

I'm skipping Ivan this Saturday and checking out the competition. Feeling this way about the lessons ain't good. Either there's something wrong with the class or there's something wrong with me. I've got to get to the bottom of this because this is not fun.

11-9: Lesson #4: So This is a Fencing School!

I check out the OTHER school in town and WOW, wadda difference! This place is clean, organized and cheerfully professional. Stately older building with a loft that holds a reception area, fencing studio, men's and lady's changing areas, etc. Equipment is in good shape. Masks, gloves and tunics are *clean* and sparkling white. Students are fresh faced and eager. I decide to sign up for the entire six-month stint and worry about the OTHER place later. I lay down the plastic in exchange for gear and I'm immediately introduced to Nestor, the instructor who is about to begin the day's lesson.

He's built like a running back and wears a genuine look of welcome. I wouldn't have picked him for a fencer (thinking of the reed thin, pasty white, aristocratic and dour stereotype that I have yet to encounter). He shakes my hand and whisks me toward the studio. I stand off to the side while he gets the class started with drills and I'm soon impressed by the man's manner and the class itself. Instructions are crisp and clear. Execution by the class is quick and sure. When Nestor sees a problem he approaches, points things out and gets the student(s) back on track without missing a beat. This guy knows what he's about and knows how to

I'm feeling this age difference thing really bad because I must seem like some wheezy old man to her. (She's 12 years old! Was I ever 12?)

communicate ...
in English!

After he gets the class initially grooved in a drill, he comes over to me and reviews from scrap all the basics sans sword: fencer's position, on guard, advance and retreat, extend and lunge. All this takes only a few minutes. Then Nestor asks a nearby student to work with me while he puts the rest of the class through a new series of drills. After a very short time (Nestor never leaves me for more than a couple minutes) he returns and has me put on my mask and pick up my sword.

We go through the same exercises with the equipment, adding parries and combinations of things until I'm rehearsing my own mini-drills. Again, his commands are easy to follow and when I need correcting, he does so quickly, kindly and smoothly.

After a bit, we go over to the practice pads attached to the wall. He calls upon a young girl to join us and to demonstrate some blade work. He has her run through some drills and it's like watching Thumbalina. She's so swift and precise! Then he has me do it. First, a simple extend and touch from on guard, then a lunge. This exercise helps me to determine distance and to develop touch technique as well as form. You want the blade to bend up in a simple ***C*** curve when you touch. I feel very comfortable with this exercise and, in fact, I think that I've been doing pretty well up to this point.

Nestor tells me to practice on my own while he goes back to the regular bunch and I soon discover that I'm really gassed. I'm HOT, very sweaty in the mask, my arms are tired and I'm wobbly on my feet. All of a sudden I'm ready for the showers. I glance at the clock and see that there's a ways to go.

After stumbling around for maybe 10 minutes, Nestor has me

come on the floor with everyone else and pairs me off with the same young gazelle who demonstrated target technique. He runs through some stuff, mostly the same as before, and has me stab at the little girl (she's about 12, I think).

OK, I'm really sweating now (the girl is fresh as a daisy) and slightly dazed. He leaves us after a brief run-through and my young friend (she's as sweet as can be) has absolutely no problem picking up the coaching mantle. She tells me to keep my torso upright, my elbow straight and a number of other things that I don't remember. I'm supposed to do a simple drill (change of engagement, extend, lunge and touch) 10 times in a row, but I never make it that far because there's always something to stop and correct. (I'm at that point where I get one thing right and forget everything else.)

I'm feeling this age difference thing really bad because I must seem like some wheezy old man to her. (She's 12 years old! Was I ever 12?) I'm thinking about being embarrassed. But before I mentally plunge, she says that I'm doing OK, that I only need to do this and that, and that I look good otherwise. I'm deeply grateful. I'm even more grateful when Nestor has us line up for some final drills without the doggone mask.

After he ends the class, Nestor asks me for some feedback (another example of his professionalism). I'm very happy to tell him that the OTHER guys don't hold a candle to his class and that I'm ecstatic to find a place where they teach fencing in English.

11-12: Lesson #5: Killjoy

I decide to confront Jack, the instructor from the OTHER school, with my decision, but he isn't there. He's out of town. Great.

Ivan is leading the class again and simply because I'm there, I decide to stay and take a lesson. There's about a dozen of us and we start with Ivan's power driven calisthenics. We tear through about 16 exercises in 4.5 minutes which, of course, is too doggone fast. Nobody's in sync and nobody's really doing the calisthenics properly at such warp speed. Ridiculous.

I raise my arms in a little victory dance and we both start laughing. But Ivan will have none of this and demonstrates a major (and unforgivable) character flaw. He's a killjoy.

We line up and work on some drills without the gear and this is OK. Advances, retreats and lunges. I enjoy working on the footwork. We all need the practice.

Next, we put on our gear and run through the same stuff with parries. I'm feeling good. This is all right.

It breaks down, however, when we pair off. My partner is new and hasn't a clue. It's difficult for him to follow stuff and the drills sorta limp along. I help as much as I can but I'm hardly ready to coach. Ivan comes along every now and then to baffle us with his explanations for things and the exercise really bogs down. At one point after a particularly incomprehensible set of instructions he asks me, "You unnerstant now?"

I'm frustrated enough to be candid: "No. I have no idea what you're talking about." He demonstrates the drill again, but it's the same old story. Between his garbled English and my ignorance, instruction is not really working. Not for me anyway.

During a break I ask one of the other students if she has trouble with Ivan's instruction. "At first I did," she replied, "but now I understand him. Of course, I'm a student of languages and perhaps it's easier for me."

There you go. Maybe I should get a masters in Russian before next Wednesday.

Eventually I pair off with the Language Lady because half the class suddenly disappears (imagine that!) and we're left without partners. Ivan asks us to bout with one another and it's the most fencing fun I've had yet. Language Lady kicks my butt (she's four months ahead of me). It's the first time I've fenced with someone who's proficient and it's exhilarating.

She tags me about six times before I finally touch her once. When I do I raise my arms in a little victory dance and we both start laughing. But Ivan will have none of this and demonstrates a major (and unforgivable) character flaw. He's a killjoy. He approaches and tells me to "take break."

He pairs me with another new student who's totally lost at sea and I've about had it. He comes over and rattles on about things and when he asks "you unnerstant?" I say "yes!" just to get the babbling Muscovite away from me.

After stumbling along with my partner for another minute, I take off my mask and say I gotta go. Driving home I bellow with frustration. Bye-bye, Ivan.

11-14: Lesson #6: Happy

Show up early at my new studio to stretch and gear up. Meet a new bunch and they're all pleasant and very helpful. All guys, different ages. Nestor arrives, takes charge promptly at 6:30 and we're off. We start with basic drills in one line: first position, salute, advances, retreats, cross-steps, thrusts and lunges. Then we pair off.

Nestor has me work with a fellow who's had about eight lessons. Dave takes me through various lunging drills that include a simple lunge, a beat (slapping the other's blade back) and lunge, a disengage (circling underneath the other's blade) with lunge and a combination disengage, advance, disengage and lunge. Each drill is broken down to fine tune my technique and eventually executed in clusters of 10 reps. It's repetitious but not horribly boring. Seems this stuff has to be drilled and drilled in order to sink in. I do OK but have a tendency to forget things after awhile. It's kinda like the golf swing: trying to remember all the parts and putting it all together in one flowing movement. It's also like learning dance steps. It's difficult for me to remember, and *keep* remembering the steps. At times my mind freezes and I screw up a drill that I've executed perfectly eight times before. I trade partners two more times and each person is as helpful and supportive as the first. This class is very big on support and communication.

> This class is very big on support and communication. Advice is freely given. A great atmosphere for learning!

Advice is freely given. A great atmosphere for learning! I need to stop every now and then to take off my mask and wipe my sweaty face.

Folks in the class run the gamut. Among them is a 30-ish computer chip guy, a 50-ish preacher type, a husky machine operator, a tall skinny teenager who is constantly fiddling with his gear and a young dead-end type kid who is eager but always doing something wrong or spastic. It's a great crew. I'm very happy here.

After class I watch the advanced group bout. Very impressive and it looks like fun. One guy has crazy legs and moves like a wild man. He's matched with a sedate looking older woman who simply shreds the guy. He moves in such a jumbled frenzy that he finally tumbles down and gets tangled in the wires that connect him to the scoring device (I want to laugh but that would be totally uncool in this place).

Action is usually lightening quick in short spurts (fencing stops after each touch and resumes immediately thereafter). Of course, each fencer is wired to a scoring device that seems to keep up with the frantic pace very well. Another student stands by as a judge. I'm still thinking the wires and everything are silly but what do I know.

11-16: Lesson #7: Bewildered

About 10 guys show. We start with drills sans gear. Hands on hips, advance, retreat, extend, lunge. Then again with arms in on guard position. And again with mask and sword. Nestor throws in parries 4 and 6 and here I'm weak.

I pair off with a more experienced student and he runs me through: simple extend and lunge, beat, extend and lunge, disengage, extend and lunge, the old one-two (step, extend, disengage and lunge) and something else that slips my mind. Each exercise is repeated 10 times with lots of constructive criticism throughout. As stated previously, nobody here is afraid to point things out!

There's so much nuance to this sport! Each tidbit of technique is simple and sensible unto itself, but that doesn't make it easy to execute properly. Taken with everything else, it gets bewildering. I struggle with remembering yesterday's tricks while learning the next new thing.

After a bit Nestor pairs off with me and puts me through the paces. I finally learn the parries 4 and 6. Four is the natural sword position and 6 is the one you gotta think about. Because it's so difficult, Nestor tells me to hold the 6 in the on guard position in order to get used to it. The other hand position for me to learn at this point (there are a few others!) is palm up (supinated) when I extend and lunge. I'm happy to finally learn these hand positions because the first school and all the books I've read have confused me. Nestor says every school and every instructor teaches things a bit differently so my confusion is not entirely of my own making.

Problems:
My lead foot has a tendency to turn in as I drill.
I roll off my back foot during the lunges.
My parries are weak.
I forget to extend before I lunge.
I sweat like a pig. Someone open the widows!

The drill with Nestor goes well and I enjoy his coaching very much. It's really great when the drills transcend the rote and a rhythm occurs (as if I know what I'm doing with a sword in my hand).

We line up for some final drills, and then two pairs of students do some actual fencing. One touch wins. The action is fast and constantly interrupted by certain judgments and scores. The judging takes longer than the action, but then Nestor is trying to teach us stuff. I can hardly follow it all, but it looks like fun and I'm eager to try a bout myself.

It's fun being dressed by a strange woman and it certainly adds to the charm of learning this exotic sport.

11-18: Lesson #8: Checking Out the Good Guys

I arrive early to order my gear. Deb, the club director/receptionist measures me for a chest guard (to wear underneath the jacket), a jacket and a glove. I also order a foil. I hope to have everything in a week. It's fun being dressed by a strange woman, and it certainly adds to the charm of learning this exotic sport. Buzz, the head guy, walks in and OKs the fitting.

Buzz, by the way, can really whale with the stick and holds a high and mighty position with the United States Fencing Association (USFA). He seems to be a friendly sort and I appreciate his comments and advice. Nestor arrives and also gives the fitting his blessing. Everyone is all smiles. Such a cheerful place!

Out on the floor we begin the usual way, and after the initial drills, we pair off. Nestor tells my guy to have me run through the same drills I've rehearsed for the last two lessons and so it goes.

After a bit, Nestor steps in and the pace gets brisk quickly. I begin to perform with less thought and every now and then it feels good. Of course, Nestor tells me when I'm on it or not, and with this guy I really try. We work on my parries 4 and 6 and they're coming around. A drill in which Nestor attacks while I parry as I retreat is especially helpful. It's always more fun and beneficial when the exercises become like bouting.

After class I watch one of the guys in my class bout with a 17-year-old woman who has qualified for some special tournament. Very enlightening. She moves economically and scores repeatedly against a stronger, more animated foe. Her swordsmanship is deft, confident and casual looking. Like she's hardly trying. It's the first time I've seen the chesslike maneuvering that I've heard about and it's very impressive. It makes me wanna try. It makes me wanna get good!

11-20: Lesson #9: My First Bout!

Eager to begin, I show up at the studio 30 minutes before class. I gear up and work on the dummy. Footwork, thrusts and lunges. The practice is paying off as I feel smoother and more confident. Got to get this stuff down so I don't have to think about it!

Class rambles on in the usual way: footwork drills without gear, hands on hips, switching feet. Then with hands up in the on guard position. Then with gear. Next we pair off and Nestor instructs each couple to work on specific drills. Tonight I'm with a young boy. Nestor instructs him to coach me through the attack drills that I've been working on for the last couple of lessons. Then Nestor steps in and runs me through the same drills at his brisk pace.

With Nestor I feel my performance improving and the drills gain a rhythm. It's almost like a bout. He's impressed that my movements are as fluid as they are. Not that I'm a picture of fencing perfection (I make lots of mistakes ... sometimes I simply fade out and forget what I'm doing) but at times it seems like I'm really getting it. At any rate, I'm enjoying myself and that's always a good indication that the instruction is going well.

After class some of the more advanced kids fence with each other. After watching the first match, I ask Nestor if I can try. I pair off with a scruffy little guy that can't be older than 12.

Now Eric is a throwback. A genuine Dead-End Kid. Quite unlike the faintly appealing yet homogenized and uninteresting mall rats that many of his peers seem to be these days. He would not be out of place, for example, in an old Our Gang comedy. I can easily picture him and Spanky plotting some wild prank to fool teachers, parents and anyone else in a position of adult authority.

Eric is a true wild man and he fences like one. After cheerfully following the precise drills of the class, he discards 90% of what he's been taught and advances upon his opponent like a pint-sized tornado. His foe tonight parries his whirlwind attack well enough at first, but can't seem to build up enough steam to create his own offense. Eric just goes and goes. He wins because he never stops

On the way home I think about the wonderful therapeutic effect of legally whaling away on a little person (take that you runt!).

attacking.

I'm next and so excited to finally be in a bout that I don't consider how amusing it must seem to everyone else. Heck, I'm 46 years old, five-nine and 170 pounds. I'm twice as big as the kid who doesn't even fill out his fencing jacket. The strap that runs through the legs hangs below his knees and his mask is stuffed with newspapers to keep it from wobbling on his head.

Nestor acts as judge and away we go. I immediately extend my arm in a thrust and break into a gallop: CHARGE! The kid reels. I score a touch and we go back to our starting points. By this time I begin to see the physical imbalance of things and think that perhaps I shouldn't press so hard. But when Nestor says "Fence!" the kid's on me in a flash swinging like a Turk. I cover up in a fetal position and start to laugh. Nestor stops the action, tells Eric to lighten up and to show some finesse.

We start again and this time I fly over. Somehow we end up banging in to each other and I can't figure out what to do at such close quarters. I hit him with the guard of my sword and since that's a no-no, action is stopped and I get a warning. As the bout goes on I end up getting more warnings for covering up with my left (non-sword) arm. It's only natural to cover up, but a fencer must learn not to give into the instinct. All the warnings end up costing me points and eventually the bout (he who gets five touches, or points first, wins).

At one time during the match Eric says he's injured. I rush over, concerned as hell, but Nestor tells Eric to stop fooling around and to get on with it. Seems the little guy is given to feigning injury in order to catch his opponent off guard. What a worm!

The match doesn't take long since both of us fence aggressively. Somehow during one exchange I step on Eric's sword and another time Eric whacks the sword right out of my hand. The latter action causes the sword to fly up and away, but I catch it and continued to fence. This drives the crowd (all four people) nuts. What a fight!

Although I lose, I managed to score four touches and pretty much had Eric on the run. In fact, after Nestor calls the match, the little guy is so dazed that he has to ask who won.

Ahh!! My first bout. What fun! On the way home I think about the wonderful therapeutic effect of legally whaling away on a little person (take that you runt!). I'm cleansed, weary and ecstatic.

11-23: Lesson #10: You Big Meany

Achy and stiff I hobble into the Saturday class. I warm up with the practice pads. We line up for the usual footwork drills sans gear, then Nestor has us suit up and we run through stuff again. We pair off and my guy has me run through the same exercises as before. Nestor comes along and sails through things in that crisp way of his.

He leaves and I pair off with another guy who shows me how to do things in the 4th position (high and inside or frontside and to my left). Up to now I've been executing only in the 6th position (high and outside or backside and to my right). Although the exercises are the same, there's a different way to hold the sword and you come in at a different angle. I have a bit of trouble with it and it doesn't help that my student/teacher is about 13 and a little confused himself.

I'm really doing poorly and at times I'm plain lost (boy, I *hate* that!). When I finally come close to getting it, the kid cries, "Good! Good! You're doin' great!" This translates to *thankgodwhatarelief* because Nestor will give him hell if I don't show improvement.

Writing this I realize that I'm not being very specific about the skills I'm learning. Maybe I should write stuff down sooner and look things up in the various texts I have. I'm afraid I forget a lot. I simply don't have a memory for this sort of thing. I'm so busy working out the specific skills that I don't record and categorize

I can't even make change. How on earth am I gonna remember all these names, numbers, drills and positions and keep my foot pointed straight at the same time?

the names of the skills I practice. It's all kind of a blur.

Not that I feel awkward. My form isn't bad. But verbalizing what I'm learning is out of reach. It seems so mathematical and regimented at times. Like memorizing the Mole Chart or something. You see, in fencing, they attach numbers and names to everything. And in my mind, real action and numbers don't mix. They don't even co-exist.

I can't even make change. How on earth am I gonna remember all these names, numbers, drills and positions and keep my foot pointed straight at the same time?

My wife, Kathleen, comes by and after class I introduce her to Nestor. I tell him how much I enjoyed sparring with little Eric the other night. I've had some time to reflect on the bout and I'm concerned that folks around here might think I pushed the kid too hard. Maybe I should feel bad about showing so much aggression (even though I lost to the runt!).

But Nestor shows no sign of discomfort as we chat so I guess everything is OK.

I'll keep an eye out for young Eric, but I won't necessarily wear the kid gloves.

11-25: Lesson #11: Study? Forgetaboutit!

Only five of us show. This makes for a more intimate class and more time with Nestor. As always we begin with basic drills and then we pair off. My partner tells me my form is very good. "You must be practicing," he says. I guess it's starting to sink in. Tonight's lesson goes quickly. It's the last before Thanksgiving. I won't have another class for a week.

Observations:
I'm getting a feel for things. I can execute the basic footwork and a lot of the basic sword play well enough. I feel the improvement and my comfort level is rising. It's fun, even the drills. I like the coaching and I definitely feel that I'm in the right place.

The problem as I see it is the memorization of all the moves. I can execute OK, but I can't readily match the names of the moves with the moves themselves. When Nestor calls them out during drills, it takes a moment for me to sort it all out in my tiny fencer's mind.

I need to keep up with the drilling, of course, and to do much more on my own. I also need to apply myself to the outside reading. I'm thinking about composing my own outline and listing all the basic techniques that we learn in class, as well as those I've discovered from the reading. The list will include a simple explanation of each move. This will force me to imprint this stuff on my brain. This is plain old studying like learning history or math formulas.

There's so much to learn mentally before I can bout instinctively. Unlike many other sports, there's a substantial foundation of knowledge that must be gained before you can play with any authority. And that's curious, isn't it? Studying or working hard at something in order to discover a glimpse of what will be fun one day. In other words, working in order to play.

Later:
Studying is a drag. I'm confused and befuddled with all the moves as they are listed and explained in each of the four books I use as references. Although there are similarities, the organization of the material is very different in each publication. There is no standard order of progression. *Forgetaboutit!*

12-2: Lesson #12: Dog of War

Only four of us show. I'm sluggish and unenthusiastic at first, but it gets better as I warm up. Drills with and without partners. Plenty of time with Nestor.

I wonder if deep down inside I'm a bloodthirsty dog of war. Has this fencing project turned loose something dark and violent in my nature?

At the end of class we have mini-matches among ourselves. Just one touch wins. Everybody fences each person in the class as well as Nestor.

I barely win my first match, win the second handily, and after an exhausting two minute bout with Nestor, I actually score against him, too.

I can't believe it! I beat everyone!

My strategy was simple: when in doubt attack! I tried toying around but felt more comfortable charging. Not that it was pretty to watch. Once I missed with a lunge and fell on my face. At one point Nestor compared my style to an enraged rhino. I'm certain the Ghosts of Fencing's Past were annoyed at my wild performances, and I'm equally sure my fellow students were taken aback as well.

But WOW! It felt so good. The blood pounds in my chest before each bout. I can hardly breathe from the excitement. So this is fencing. Cool.

I assumed Nestor let me touch him, but he says no, that I caught him off guard somehow. He says he let up when he saw me stop at one point in exhaustion and that I chose that moment to give it one last try. He also says that luck plays a big part in fencing. At any rate, it's safe to say that Nestor can skewer me at will if he has the notion. He was fooling around trying to get us to respond with the moves he had just taught us.

After my bouts Nestor has me judge one of the matches. The action is so swift that I find it hard to keep up. I'm supposed to halt the action when there's a score, a mis-hit or a violation, but half the time it blows by me. Judging is fun and interesting, though, and a great way to learn.

On the way home I'm so pumped that I bellow along with the

radio (Van Halen). I wonder if deep down inside I'm a bloodthirsty dog of war. Has this fencing project turned loose something dark and violent in my nature? They call this the Gentleman's Sport, but that ain't how I feel now. Black flag!

12-5: Lesson #13: Coming Back Down

About a dozen show. After the usual routines, I pair off with the guy who looks like a priest.

If nothing else this guy can do a salute that really shines. You can tell he loves doing it. Standing at attention, ram rod straight and imperious, making the swishing sound with his weapon. He actually told me once that he took up lessons because he enjoyed the aura and ritual of traditional fencing. He pretends he's a musketeer or something. It's pretty funny. I can picture this guy at home in front of the mirror saluting himself with pomp.

After awhile Nestor had us switch partners and I end up with a friendly young fellow who I've worked with before. He's been fencing for about a year and looks very good. He doesn't hesitate to tell me my mistakes, which is quite all right with me.

Nestor closes the class with some one-touch mini-bouts and my opponent is the newest kid in class. I'm thinking that I caused such a commotion last time that I'd cool it tonight. I'm afraid if I keep attacking like a wild man that no one will want to fence with me.

Nestor says, "Fence!" and the new kid springs into action while I remain still. He sorta taps my blade but I don't move a muscle. Finally I advance and whack here and there at his sword thinking that I'm showing alotta control and style. Then in an instant he touches me and it's over. Nuts.

I stay to watch two of the more seasoned fencers. They attach themselves to a scoring device and go at it. The action is furiously contained in 10 second bursts of fighting that stops when someone scores. The fencing resumes almost immediately so there's hardly a break in the action. It looks like they fence until they drop.

... it's hard to feel good about yourself when some 12-year-old thinks you're a pussy.

Nestor comes over and tells me that it takes about six months to get to the point where you're fencing with real know-how like these guys. Until then you're just whaling away. He says that I'm on track and progressing well. "At least you didn't fall down tonight," he says and we both laugh.

12-7: Lesson #14: Pussy Boy

Saturday's class is full. The younger ones show so it's animated. The kids are very helpful and take the time to show the old man (me) how it's done. I'm grateful that they even pay attention. I'm a little off today (maybe because I spent the morning surfing) and Nestor actually laughs at my stumbling around. It's not a problem because it's so funny (and he certainly isn't trying to be malicious). Heck, I'm laughing, too.

At one point during the drills, Nestor instructs the class to execute a series of parries while retreating several steps. The whole class, except me, falls back in perfect formation. For some reason I can't get my mind to focus on the job at hand (now how does that go again?) and I'm left standing there in stupid wonder. As everyone stares I start laughing again. Nestor says something about working at your own pace, and I say that that would require a very long lesson indeed (more laughs).

I end up working with three younger folks who show me the right way to execute the parries 4, 6, 7 and 8. They get into a little debate and it's cute the way they want me to get it right.

Near the end of class, one of the kids is picked to fence one-touch with everyone in the class. Nestor wants him to experience different styles, one after the other. When my turn comes I start out cautiously (this is my strategy) and I let myself get backed up. I attack after awhile and I think I touch, but the hit is deemed flat (hitting with the side of the blade versus the point).

We return to on guard and resume the battle. Again I think I score, but again I'm wrong as the class judges that it's actually I who gets touched. Reasons are given that fly over my head. My young opponent takes off his mask and gives me a pointer. "Don't freak out when I attack," he says while he mimics my (apparently) frenzied retreat in front of the entire class.

I guess he thought my cautious strategy was born of fear. I'm slightly dismayed *(but, but, I'm not a coward!!)* although I don't say anything. We pack it up soon after and I try to keep a good spin on the lesson ... but it's hard to feel good about yourself when some 12-year-old thinks you're a pussy.

12-9: Lesson #15: Animal

God I love this game!

Another round of one-touch bouts after class tonight. Somehow I'm the one everyone gets to fence and it's a total charge. I fence all five students plus Nestor and whip all but one. I even beat Nestor again! Unbelievable.

The first guy is new and I barely get by him. The second fellow I tag with a quick attack that's gotta be luck. The next guy runs me off the strip initially, but the split second we reengage I charge hard and plant one on his chest. The class whoops it up and laughs as does Nestor, but he says that I fleched (full body tilt, spring loaded push-off, both feet off the ground, near horizontal rocket launch) and that because we haven't covered it yet, I shouldn't do it. (I have no idea that I'm executing such an involved maneuver. I'm only trying to get to him before he gets to me!)

Then I bout with a young lady who is actually quite skillful and graceful. But I'm rolling now and tag her with what looks like a groin hit (which count). I'm thinking she's gotta be hurtin' (I would be) but she shrugs it off. Next up is the biggest guy in class. I do fine for a bit but I eventually get touched and it's all over.

Finally Nestor comes to bat. He immediately puts me on the defensive by sticking his twirling foil in my face and leaving it there like a giant angry bee that won't go away. I whack at it and do a couple of attacks but it's like scaling Fort Knox at high noon.

> I'd like to become a good defensive fencer. It seems to me if you could ward off the attack, you would be invincible. So often, though, the bout becomes a blur of action/reaction and using strategy is impossible.

Then, miraculously, I penetrate and plant the tip on his chest. It's exhilarating but I know Nestor could slice me up for lunch if he had a mind to.

I do my best at these things when I'm on offense. I look for a weakness (an open line, a lazy sword, an incomplete attack) and simply attack with an advance and lunge. Sometimes I lay back and wait, trying a retreat/parry type thing if my opponent is cautious.

I'd like to become a good defensive fencer. If you could ward off the attack, you would be invincible. So often, though, a bout becomes a blur of action/reaction and using strategy is impossible.

I think I'm doing OK, but I know sometimes I'm loosing it by making clumsy advances (and clumsy retreats) and swinging my sword in wide, inefficient arcs. Nestor always says that *it looks better than it feels* but I know he wants me to pace myself better and build up to each attack. At any rate, I'm doing a lot right and Nestor says so.

After the bouts, one of the guys smiles and calls me an an animal. It's a compliment, of course, and it makes me feel good, but it's not like I'm trying to be a mad man. I'm only trying to survive out there!
Nestor makes it happen. His attitude, know-how and control of the class is impeccable. During all of the above he gives a running analysis of what's going on, who's doing what and who should work on what. His enthusiasm and encouragement dominates, keeping things loose and light in contrast to the furious activity of our flaying swords. He's a remarkable coach.

Of course, I'm very high about the night and thrilled that I should be singled out to fence everybody. I've seen Nestor give others the same treatment and I'm sure he'll spread it around as time goes on. I'm certain that he's got a plan.

The classes always go lightening quick. We start out with some basic drills, without and then with sword. Then we pair off to run through more drills. The drills are the same yet something new is always added. Nestor visits each one of us during the pairing drills to give a little one-on-one. In no time 45 minutes pass and it's time for the mini-bouts.

Sampling of drill exercises:

Without sword:
With hands on hips: advances, retreats, cross-steps forward and backward and lunges. Reverse feet and direction (opposite foot forward) and repeat. Same with hands behind back. Same with arms in the on guard position. Nestor runs us through the drills himself then has us run through them on our own in two-minute increments.

With sword:
Same as above (switching sword hands is tricky!) with parries 4, 6, 7 and 8. Again, Nestor runs us through the drills himself, then has us run through them on our own in two-minute increments.

The foundation for everything is footwork. The drills pound in the fundamentals and smooth out form. Obviously, you want to get this stuff down to muscle memory so you don't have to think about it. There is no time during a bout or even an advanced drill to think about your hands and feet!

Drills with partners:
Simple thrusts, disengage thrusts, beats and thrusts, presses, one-twos, doubles and parries. Partners are encouraged to critique each other, especially the more advanced students helping the new. Advice is given and taken freely and in good spirit. At this time the new moves are introduced. This is also when Nestor goes around and instructs each student in quick, no-nonsense lessons/drills gauged to each student's level of expertise. It's noteworthy that Nestor can do that and keep an eye on everyone

I've come to look forward to class and approach each lesson with a single-mindedness that up to this point has been reserved for only surfing, bill collecting and sex.

else's progress at the same time. Nobody is ever left standing around without a directive. Class is a clean machine.

Classes are usually small, never more that 10 strong. This makes for an intimacy, camaraderie and spirit worth coming back for three times a week. I've come to look forward to class and approach each lesson with a single-mindedness that up to this point has been reserved for only surfing and bill collecting.

12-18: Lesson #16: Showing Me How

I missed two lessons because of an out-of-town trip. I show about 6 p.m. to warm up slowly and practice on my own. After preliminary drills I'm paired with a young fellow who's got the goods and is not afraid to tell me I don't.

He puts me through the paces, breaking down everything I do. I have problems keeping my arm extended during my lunges, my tip pointed properly and disengaging in small circles. All his criticisms are right on.

I kept bending my arm because my advances were too long in the step, putting me too close to my opponent. I begin to judge distance better and to gauge my advances accordingly. This cures the extension problem.

The tip problem is cured by pointing the tip in slightly (in the 6th line) during the lunge. This ensures that the blade will stick to my target and not slip off.

Correcting the disengage is again a matter of judging the distance better and using my fingers to rotate the tip instead of my hand and arm. With my giant steps I was putting myself too close to my opponent and his sword. In order to circle around his sword and arm I had to create large circles. By keeping distance, I can move my tip around his tip with a lot less motion.

Then I get paired with a young woman who has some talent but is somewhat shy about coaching. I still feel too humble to impart criticism and expect everyone else to show the way. We spend too much time wondering what to do with each other so I make an excuse and take a breather. Upon reflection I guess I should have tried harder to make something happen. After all, I am older. Shouldn't I be more patient and constructive?

My little lesson with Nestor jolts me out of my doldrums. We go a bit beyond the drills and almost get into a bouting-like thing. He advances and attacks, I advance and attack, and he throws in some unexpected moves. Alotta fun.

Then we do some one-touch bouts and guess who wins? I can't really say how I do it, but I make the touches and do so very cleanly. I feel more in control but that could be an illusion. I can't tell you how much fun it is to bout ... and win!

12-21: Lesson #17: Wonderkid Workout

After drills I pair off with the tall kid with the bothersome gear. After that ho-hum session, I pair with Mark the Wonderkid. He's about 14, a little short, wears glasses, very articulate and good with the blade. We go through basic thrusts, disengages, one-twos, doubles, beat attacks and some newer moves that include feints and ripostes.

Mark plays the coach as usual (I let everyone coach me. I really don't feel comfortable playing that role. But I also have a selfish reason. The "student" gets more practice than the "coach"). Mark is fun and helpful. He likes to mix it up, too. To get away from the monotony of the drills, he does something unexpected every now and then so I learn to react to an opponent versus simply following a drill. This kind of practicing can simulate a real bout.

Very soon it seems (class time really flies) the class is nearly over and Nestor has us bout each other. Again, I do very well in my

Offense comes naturally: charging and whaling away like a kid. Defense is different. It takes a more measured, patient response.

matches. After class I fence full five-touch bouts with Mark and another fellow who is quite good. I lose but I do well enough, giving both a fight. More importantly, I understand what I need to improve.

Offense comes naturally: charging and whaling away like a kid. Defense is different. It takes a more measured, patient response. And that's hard to do when the other guy is coming on strong. It's only natural to fight back. But what you want to do is carefully parry the attacks, watch your opponent's moves and wait for the offensive opportunity to present itself. You gotta keep your head!

During the bouts I get frustrated with my lack of skill and inability to defend myself or break through my opponent's defenses. I shout, "I know there's something I should be doing here!" or "Nuts! I can't break through!" Not that I'm mad, really. Just stymied. On cue, Nestor calls a halt, tells me a thing or two and we start again. Always the watchful head coach.

It's all great fun in the end. I feel myself growing more accustomed to the swordplay. I realize what a great advantage it is to be a good parrier. Mark tells me it's all concentration. Focus on the action!

We take turns judging each other's matches. It's difficult because the action is so fast, even with beginners, and hard to discern what actually happens. As soon as a touch, miss or foul occurs, the judge must call a halt and say what's what. It takes a sharp eye, a sure memory and a quick mind to capsulize the action.

I'm almost worthless as a judge. I can't see without my glasses (I don't wear them because they fog up), and I'm painfully slow following the action and calling a halt when something happens. When it comes to explaining the sequence of events leading up to the reason for calling the halt, forget it! I end up calling the touches without explanation or asking the guys if they thought they'd been touched. But no one complains (such a good spirited bunch) and everybody assures me that it takes time.

12-23: Lesson #18: Doing Fine with Alaska Dave

Last class before holiday break. And only two other students show! This promises to be an intense session.

Start with usual warm-up. Then I pair off with a more experienced fellow whom I've bouted with previously. He's rather talented. And big. We run through the routine and it's good because he's good and willing to "coach" (sometimes it gets boring and sloppy with other students because neither of us knows what to do).

Next I get a thorough session with Nestor. We follow the drills up to a point, but it gets more substantial very quickly. Some stuff I follow with my mind, but the rest I hope sinks in on its own somehow. Nestor picks up on my self-flagellation and tells me that it'll come ... I'm doing fine.

Before I let him go I ask him how to parry (what I call) his *in-your-face-twirling-tip* attack. He does exactly that every time I've gone against him and it's totally baffling. He chuckles and says that I must learn to step back when the attack comes ... not to simply stand there. He goes on about parries and lines of attack but it flies over my head like most of this stuff usually does when I first hear it. He sees my mild dismay and once again says not to worry. It'll come together in time.

My first match is with the big guy. It's very close and I lose by a hair. We've bouted before and it's alotta fun. We're both somewhat aggressive and prone to fits of weed whacking.

My next opponent is from Alaska. He's a bit more experienced. In fact, I don't think he's a student. Just sorta stopping by or something. He moves like he knows a thing or two, but, the thing is, he wears fencing britches so he's gotta be a player!

We start to fence and right away I notice a difference in the guy's style. He's very cautious. At first he simply stands there. He lets me

... the fencing world is still quite small. You can get out there and cross swords with the very best at a given match. Imagine trying to do that in tennis!

attack. He easily parries everything I throw at him and shows very little aggression. This goes on for some time and finally he simply reaches out and touches me. Afterward, he tells me that he tried to keep his moves simple, doing things that I'd be familiar with. He also tells me that proficiency will come. Maybe not fast enough for me, but in time.

This was a good session. Having that extra attention is great. After the holidays I'll ask Nestor for one private lesson a week.

1-3: Saber Night (Thursday is not Wednesday)

I show up thinking it's Wednesday, my regular foil night. It's actually Thursday (am I in a fog or what?), saber night, but I hang out anyway because I've been wanting to check it out.

There's only two guys in the class and I watch Nestor put them through the drills. It's a little different than foil. They bang each other on the top of their masks a lot. They hold and swing the thing differently as well. It's a bit more swashbuckling, like the movies. More slash and less thrust.

But it's boring just watching. I'm used to working up quite a lather. I talk to Susan, Buzz's wife (he's the owner) as she drops by to check the bulletin board for competitions. I've seen her fence and she looks really good to me. She tells me about a recent competition where she faced Olympians although she is not rated or ranked very high. Apparently this is not so strange because the fencing world is still quite small. You can get out there and cross swords with the very best at a given match. Imagine trying to do that in tennis! She even encourages me to enter a competition. I laugh and say I've hardly begun, but Alaska Dave who's standing nearby says, "*Heck, that's how ya learn! So what if ya lose!*"

I sign up for an extra private session per week (20 minutes) with Nestor. I tell him I'm already showing up three times a week. He laughs and says I'm only allowed two classes per week according to the program, but not to worry. He likes to see lots of bodies in his classes and I think he really digs my enthusiasm. Whatever. I need to accelerate the process, and if I need to spend more money, so be it!

1-4: Lesson #19: Alaska Dave, Green Legs and Getting Undressed

The first foil class after the holidays is surprisingly small. About six of us show. The usual: drills sans sword, drills with sword, drills with partners. Nestor keeps an eye on everybody and advises each pair of fencers according to need and skill level. I know he likes to teach large groups. I think he's proud of his ability to successfully manage many students. It's a challenge for him and he's quite good at it.

The bouting begins after about 40 minutes. I try to incorporate tact and some of the new skills I've been taught as opposed to just charging. I would really like to have more control out there. I lose most of my matches, but every now and then I pull off something smooth. Like anticipating my opponent's next move, finding the opening and making the deft touch.

I especially enjoy my bouts with David (Alaska Dave), Nestor and the Big Guy (we also call him Danny Green Legs because he always wears green sweats). David is very tactful and his style makes me slow down and think, which is good. I actually anticipate one of his moves and score. He tags me time and time again, however, and twice he touches during a falling back retreat after I attack and miss. It reminds me of a fadeaway in basketball. Very nifty.

Of course my matches with Nestor are always fun. I try the twirling tip attack on him this time and actually make a touch. He ends up creaming me, but I score twice.

The Big Guy is a challenge because he has a long reach. If I miss during an attack, it's very easy for him to simply reach out and

I get a charge out of simply pulling off a move or two. A decent parry ... a solid attack ... measured responses as opposed to mere flailing ...

touch. Again I look for the patterns, trying to concentrate and think on my feet. It's very difficult because the action is so fast and my skill level is so low.

I referee a couple of the bouts and rediscover what a great way it is to learn the sport. A judge must not only follow the action, but also be able to articulate the action. It takes a clear mind, a focused eye and a skillful command of the tongue.

You really have to concentrate in order to do all that and make fast decisions. As soon as you see a touch or a foul, you have to halt the match and describe the action leading up to that touch or foul. Since the sport is so doggone fast and the fencers so eager to reengage, a judge must be able to spit out the play-by-play without hesitation. I'm so bad that even the guys fencing have to help me out! But that's how you learn and everyone is very supportive and patient with my efforts.

1-8: Lesson #20: My First Private

Sick this week. Missed Monday's class. I don't feel much better tonight, but since we're off to Hawaii for a week, I feel I gotta show tonight. I'm glad I did!

Although I'm a little foggy, I get through the preliminary drills and by the time we pair off, I'm actually feeling better. My partner (aka Van Dyke because of his beard) is newer than I and not real hip to the tricks ... but not bad either. My groggy mood is helpful somehow. Making me a little more patient. The drills with Van Dyke get better with practice.

Nestor doesn't get to us before class ends, and to make up for it, lets me bout everyone in class. I make a point of making calculated moves. I try out the stuff we've been drilling. I attempt to scope the other guy's moves. I want to *fence*. Not just run 'em over. I care a bit less about winning.

I get a charge out of simply pulling off a move or two. A decent parry ... a solid attack ... measured responses as opposed to mere flailing ... beat attacks ... the twirling sword thing that Nestor does, sticking the extended weapon in the face ... timing the attack ... backing up during my parries (I still like to hold my ground). I win some and lose a couple, but I fence with sensibly throughout and I'm very pleased.

Tonight was my first private with Nestor. It's great. A very accelerated learning experience. He's such a good coach and I follow him well. We cover familiar territory and work on combos of things. The drills begin to blend with what must be real fencing and it's exhilarating. Especially when the give-and-take occurs: attack, parry, riposte, counter-riposte. He has me work on something where I control the opponent's sword, pushing it down and coming off it to lunge and attack. We work on variations where I hold, attack, he parries, I parry and riposte. It's only a 20-25 minute lesson, but he has me really go at it and it's more than enough.

Making the connections with the drills during a bout and the lessons with Nestor is totally aces! They're less marching orders and more a fluid exchange. It comes together in the briefest of instances and it's such a discovery. Like: oh yeah! I get it now!

1-20: Lesson #21: Stabbed in the Brain?

First day back from vacation. My hand and arm begin to ache early and I wheeze a bit. Funny how, despite a week of physical activity (surfing), I can still be out of shape for fencing.

Only three students show including me. One of the students is the under-20 champion of the region, and she's alotta fun to drill with. We do some of the rote drills and then we get into some exchanges to practice parries. It gets very close to bouting.

The small class allows a lot of time with Nestor. The drills give way to exchanges. The boutlike action with running instruction is exhilarating and a great learning experience. I feel the drills and

Making the connections with the drills during a bout and the lessons with Nestor is totally aces! They're less marching orders and more a fluid exchange

the lessons translating into real action and response. I feel the proper reflexes forming. My thinking and reflexes are more fluid and working together.

We bout as usual toward the end of class. I fence with Van Dyke. At first it's a stalemate as we both simply charge and hack with no finesse. Then I make myself think and I begin to put it together. I score five straight touches.

Next I fence the young lady who is so much more deft than I. She's very calculating and cautious until she's sees her opening and then bingo! I find myself flatfooted at times (not retreating enough) and my parries are weak. I put up a good fight and score one nice touch. She gets five on me but the quality of the bout is so high that my loss is no big deal.

Actually I find myself more into earning the clean touch (not lucky, ungainly hacks or stabs) and executing snappy parries. Merely winning these tiny fights is a little less important now. Overall form and execution with thought is my new concern. If I get one cool and calculated move or series of moves in a match, I'm happy. What's winning if it's only luck, wild swinging, intimidation or pure force and speed? After all, I'm developing now and it's the learning turning into real reflexes that's important. Using my head. Becoming a *fencer.*

Nestor gets on a little soapbox and tells about the dangers of fencing. He talks about competitors who got stabbed in the leg and in the face. He talks about a guy who got stabbed ... in the *brain.* And died. I'm open mouthed. I almost laugh because it sounds so ... unlikely. But he says it can happen if fencers don't continually check their gear.

I have no fear in this sport. Combat with swords doesn't bother me at all. It's nothing like a steep slope, a big wave or even a windy day on a sailboat. But bad things can happen if a mask is rusty or a blade snaps. I guess it's easy to forget that the sword your opponent is wielding is propelled with some force ... if equipment is faulty, you can get hurt.

Nestor closes by saying it's a mistake to think that fencing is a delicate pursuit.

1-22: Lesson #22: Flattered, Battered and Blind

I pair off with one of my favorite partners, Mark. He puts me through old drills plus some new that include work in the low line positions of 7 and 8. The swordhand positions are awkward and actually cramp my hands. We do OK and I get to that point where the drilling gains rhythm. Mark also likes to throw in changes during the drills so that I learn to fence the fencer and not merely perform drills. He's a very good teacher despite his young age and we enjoy our camaraderie.

During the one-touch bouts at the end of class (we've dispensed with the final drills, thank goodness!) I try to incorporate new skills, lay back and think through the matches. I do very well using less of the beating, straight thrust and more with feints and attacks/ripostes off circular parries. As I face off with Mark, who always beats me, I throw him a little smack for laughs: "Are you ready to get beat? Tonight's the night, pal!" Everybody cracks up because as a rule nobody *ever* says stuff like that around here.

But to his credit Nestor says, "Hey, that's cool. It's supposed to be fun!" and away we go. (I think of my first instructor, Ivan the Russian, who made me "Take Break!" after my harmless "victory dance" in November. Now there's a contrast!)

But Mark makes short work of me because I root to a spot during his attacks and forget to back the heck up. There's a tendency among many of us to stand fast during attacks and to muscle the other guy's sword. Like Earl Flynn, we think we're gonna brace against each other's charge and then hurl him away with a flick of the wrist. What really happens is that we loose our distance when we forget to retreat and become sitting ducks against another attack or riposte.

I throw him a little smack for laughs: "Are you ready to get beat? Tonight's the night, pal!" Everybody cracks up because as a rule nobody <u>ever</u> says stuff like that around here.

I finally fence with Alaska Dave, and after toying with me for a while, he lets me have it. Actually, he lets me run into a trap as he has figured my pattern of play. David has years of fencing under his belt and losing, of course, is a given against him and nothing to be ashamed of. What's important and helpful is his advice, which he gives freely without patronage.

I'm bushed at this point, sweating like a horse and wondering how I'm gonna get through my private with Nestor. Actually, I had a round with him earlier and could hardly keep up then. I give myself five minutes and we start. Again the drills give way to combinations of things in the 4 and 6 lines and then the 7 and 8. A rhythm is established (thanks to Nestor) and I work on beat attacks, one-twos, doubles, parry-ripostes, retreats ... all the stuff. Not in drill fashion where it's anticipated, but under boutlike conditions where I need to study his moves and time my responses. Afterward Nestor compliments my efforts and my rhythm. I think he's over-complimenting me because I feel clumsy. But he says, "It always *looks better than it feels*. And I don't hand out false flattery."

Puffed with the kind words, we shake and I start to pack it in when Mark comes over to ask for a match. I say sure and we fence two five-touch bouts ... and I win them both! So easily that I ask him if he's trying. He says he is, but I can see that he's tired. Nevertheless, I'm flying because I fenced him so well and finally beat the guy.

Truly flagged at this point, I undress and look for my glasses. One of the better fencers in the club comes over and says that Debbie has them, and that he squashed them with his equipment case. (These guys travel with a set of swords and tools in a small trunk). He has a ring in his eyebrow, which I can't keep my eyes off of as he apologizes. I say no worries and hand in my jacket. I discover that my glasses are totally bent with the lens popped out. Oh well. I order another jacket from Deb, since the original model I requested will probably never show, stumble to my van and drive home tired, elated and blind.

1-25: Lesson #23: Tattooed

Saturday's class has about a dozen students. We start off with old drills (to accommodate those who attend less often) and pair off. I practice with a 15-year-old version of Bill Gates. He even talks like I imagine the computer tycoon would talk. He's kinda eggheady, but nice and, like all the other kids, dwells on telling me what to do.

The bouts are fun (they're always fun) and I continue to try new things and contemplate my actions. I score off some circular parries that feel good and actually lose only once. The winner is a young, athletic man who has tattoos, blazing reflexes and isn't very wild considering he's (I think) new. I think I scored a touch before he did, but the judges didn't see it that way. He is *fast*. I felt in control and enjoyed the bout nevertheless. I'm looking forward to fighting him again!

1-27: Lesson #24: Green Legs Goes Down

We work on compound attacks after a few basic drills. I team with Danny Green Legs. He with the reach another six inches greater than mine. Fencing with him is a real challenge, but a heck of a lot of fun.

We bout until eight. I finally beat Green Legs! This guy usually wins because of his experience and reach, but tonight I score well off my circling sword. There's a name for these things, but it's all a blur in my mind. I only know that it feels right. I seem to land the touches when I riposte, continue the attack and catch him on a backpedal. It's tough because with a simple arm extension he can score easily. Even when he's stumbling back.

Victory was very sweet ... and I tell him so. HA!
This, of course, riles him and he asks (demands) for a rematch. We go at it, and like the first match it's neck and neck (we go to five

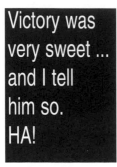

Victory was very sweet ... and I tell him so. HA!

touches). At 4 to 4 we replay two touches: one touch because it's a simultaneous hit and another because it's unclear who has priority. Can't get much closer than that! Green Legs finally scores on a very clean circular action off my blade. Too much fun!

1-29: Lesson #25: From Drills to Magic

Only three of us show. Can't believe it. Mark is my partner tonight and Nestor has us work on low line (7 and 8) attacks, parries and ripostes. This is very hard on the hand. Awkward. I'm used to the high line (6 and 4). A little practice is needed here.

I get a lot of attention from Nestor in class and during my private lesson. I continue to go in and out of understanding, but he says it's coming along. No problem.

The bouts are fun. I hang back and work on parries until Nestor makes me riposte. It comes together during the matches. I feel very confident. I try to incorporate the lessons with the bouting, and it's a real rush when it works.
Learning this stuff has two distinct stages so far:

1) The LESSON where each skill is introduced, explained and drilled (endlessly and forever, again and again like a mantra or a ritual).

2) And then there's the MAGIC. When you execute the skills without thinking. When it becomes reflex. Muscle memory takes over so your brain can focus on the actions of your opponent. You can save all your mental prowess to plot the demise of your opponent.

2-1: Lesson #26: Poor Sport

My head isn't into the lesson. I actually sneak out of class at one point because I'm so out of it.

Still sluggish during the bouts. And worse, I'm a poor sport, arguing over touches (a big no-no). I feel ashamed of myself. I'm sure some of the guys are a little put out with my behavior (what a jerk!).

I get touched twice in the groin, but no damage. I'm wearing my cup from now on.

2-2: Regional Tournament

The match is held at Mission Bay High School in San Diego. Maybe 50 or 60 fencers and fans are milling about. Not a big draw. I see my friend Mark sitting in the bleachers looking dejected, and I sit next to him. He says he just finished a round (his first in competition) and got creamed. He's depressed about his performance. He's been at it for a year and he thinks he should be better. I try to cheer him up. Looking around at those fencing, I say it appears that everyone is real good and that he shouldn't feel bad about losing his first time around. It takes courage just to get out there and try! I don't think it helps much.

There are three or four bouts going on at the same time in different areas of the gym. Most of the judges are competitors themselves. It's a very chummy bunch. Matches are fast and furious. I barely follow the action. They start, and a point is scored within seconds. They bout to five and it's over in a minute or two. Even after all my lessons I couldn't tell someone what I'm seeing.

The judging is truly awesome. These people totally control the action and describe the action after every halt. Sure, they have an electric device to help keep track of touches, but they still must know what led up to the score and be able to describe all the movements right after they occur. They really know their stuff! They analyze and spit it out in nano seconds.

I stay for about an hour. I see certain people win a lot at saber and foil. Of course, I understand the foil a little better than the saber. The latter is a charging sport. Seems the first to react wins. Foil is more structured.

Overall, it's like a big family picnic. Most everyone is involved and the only spectators are Moms and a few Dads. Things happen

And then there's the MAGIC. When you do the skills without thinking. When it becomes reflex. Muscle memory takes over so your brain can focus on the actions of your opponent.

really quick and efficiently. Some competitors shout or groan but there's no arguing or ill will. I can see how an outsider would find the scene strange. The outfits are kinda alien looking and the action is incomprehensible. It's not like you can tell right away who wins and loses. It's a real insider's thing.

2-5: Lesson #27: Getting a Big Head

Two carrot headed young men (aka The Twins) and Van Dyke show tonight. Regular drills. Some new stuff. Van Dyke and I sorta make up drills to make it more interesting.

During the class bouts I feel a little out of it, but Nestor tells me I'm doing very well. He's impressed with one of my actions. A circular thingy that he tells me is a hit in opposition. Taking the opponent's blade on a disengage and sliding mine in for the touch.

My private with Nestor is the best yet. We work on that opposition thing from the 4th position. When it works, it's very cool because you're holding the other guy's blade off while making the touch. It's like an offensive move with a defense built in.

I think all the studying I did today concerning epee (I'm still doing some outside reading) sunk in a little. Epee is all about scoring in opposition because there is no right of way. You are vulnerable when attacking unless you can "take" the other guy's blade.

Nestor takes me aside and tells me that I have what it takes. "I don't usually say this because I don't want to give students a big head. But you're a natural. A fighter," he says. I'm totally stoked, of course. Wow.

2-8: Lesson #28: Being Nice

We work on taking the blade. The same thing Nestor had me work on last time. It works so well in practice!

In the bouts after class, I lose to Green Legs and Alaska Dave. Green Legs does this thing where he parries going back. Of course, he has a reach to China that should be illegal. Dave is more my size but very skilled. He has this trick where he cranks around my parry 4. Obviously I'm not holding my parry over far enough. I feel out of control at times and I wish my skills were better (what else is new!).

I make a concerted effort to be "nice" and joke about being a "good sport, at least for today." No one seems to be holding a grudge about my behavior last Wednesday. Maybe it's all in my head. But I make the effort because I don't want to cultivate bad vibes.

2-10: Lesson #29: Slump

A rainy night. Only Danny Green Legs and I show. Nestor is in one of his disappearing modes ("I'll be in the workshop if you need me"). We laugh it off and amuse ourselves. Dan is a good student and a great partner. We work on hits in the opposition and things sorta spill over into other things. The hits in opposition are tricky because it's hard to keep the blade tight against the other in order to keep it deflected.

Later, we bout up a storm and I lose, lose, lose. Seems I'm in a slump. I'm not making the smooth moves .... forgetting to parry ... getting hit with simple attacks to my chest. Nestor says I'm too concerned with scoring, and he's right. I fence Nestor and do much better. First, he's not as tall as Dan, so the reach factor isn't so warped. Second, he's not a thrasher and I'm not pulled into a slam-bang bout. Third, I know he's holding back.

2-12: Lesson #30: What?

Not a good night. We work that opposition thing and it's all Greek to me. I get confused with the instructions (numbers, lines and labels!). Working with the kids is a real drag. I let them coach (as usual), but they're fairly confused themselves (yet sharper than

I can see how an outsider would find the scene strange. The outfits are kinda alien looking and the action is incomprehensible.

me). This opposition stuff is simple yet difficult to get right. I feel so clumsy!

2-15: Lesson #31: Tattoo You

Mark teaches me some takings of the blade in new positions. He learned them from his privates with Buzz. I dig these maneuvers.

During the mini-bouts after drills, I finally beat Tattoo (he with the blazing reflexes). Decisively!

Soon after my bout with Tattoo begins, I notice the patterns in his approach. I have a plan to circle around his point as he does this twirly thing every once in awhile. I'm sure I can counter his motion and score. I'm ready to pounce when Nestor stops the match to ask me if I see it. A little put out, I say, "Yeah, and I was ready to bushwhack him, too." Nestor backs off and lets us resume (poor Tattoo must be thinking he's being set up ... and he is!). Sure enough, Tattoo makes that little move and bingo, I make the hit.

This game is such a trip. It's such a mind game. Noticing that opening and placing the point was like threading a needle. So much more satisfying than a lucky hit. It's the best I've ever fenced.

Mark and I fence and I beat him, too. After class he asks for another bout and he destroys me. What's with this guy? In front of people he wilts, but with no one watching he turns into Zorro. Go figure.

2-17: Lesson #32: Feeding Steel!

Only Danny Green Legs and I show up. Nester once again disappears into his workshop, and the two of us shoot the breeze. (I'm starting to think that Nestor is disappearing on purpose. That maybe he wants us to relax during a lesson every once and awhile. It's not a bad idea. There's a tendency to get intense and perhaps backing off a bit is good for restoring the camaraderie and fun.)

We bout later. I especially like the bouting/lesson approach where Nestor stops the action occasionally to impart pointers. It combines the thrill of the fight with the learning. So much better than drills!

Nestor has these dramatic phrases to describe hits or touches that really crack me up. Like *Feeding Steel*. "If you leave your line open, your opponent will feed steel." Sounds so menacing and literary. Like something out of *The Count of Monte Cristo*. (Ah, Nestor, you're such a showman!)

2-19: Lesson #33: Making It Pop!

I pair off with Mark and we go through a number of drills. He directs as usual. Nestor and I have good workouts during class and during the private. I bout with one of The Twins and Mark and it's fun. It's so cool when the fight is a real fencing match and not a whirlwind affair (actually not many of those anymore).

The private is very good. Working on takings of the blade, timing, feel ... *form*. So much of fencing after a certain point is *nuance*. The techniques are not so complicated once you get beyond the language and the numbers. It's the execution, the deft touch that comes more slowly. When to make it pop! When to slow it down and speed it up. Quite often I'm in a hurry and the rushing screws up my form.

2-22: Lesson #34: Gotta Beat Green Legs

Drills with Danny Green Legs are good because we know each other, our skills are comparable (he's better) and he has a ready laugh. We like to goof on Nestor when he's in Workshop Mode (he likes to disappear with us especially. Are we that good or that bad?)

Kathleen shows up and watches me beat Tattoo (yeah!) and get beat by Green Legs. Afterward she tells him that I lie awake at night and mutter, "I gotta beat Green Legs!" over and over. Very funny.

This game is such a trip. It's such a mind game. Noticing that opening and placing the point was like threading a needle. So much more satisfying than a lucky hit.

Dan tells us about a club he's in that meets in large numbers and stages medieval battles. They wear armor and clout each other with rattan weapons. Sometimes the teams are hundreds strong. Sounds like *Braveheart* or something pretty close to it. Wild.

2-24: Lesson #35: I'm Glad You're Improving, But I Still Wanna Kick Your Butt

Drills with Van Dyke are getting better because he's getting better. I've really noticed his improvement. Good for him.

Mini-bouts: I beat Green Legs, he beats me. Others are coming along very well. They're catching up. A guy who was out for six weeks whales! Van Dyke is reaching a another plateau and has become a challenging opponent.

I'm still concerned about winning, but how can that be bad? I try not to be a wuss when I lose. It's especially difficult if I don't agree with the calls.

We go at it until 8:30. The camaraderie is improving with skill level. The game really is a balance of aggression, fair play and good sportsmanship. I mean, you see these guys all the time and you wanna get along, but you also wanna kick their butts! It makes for an interesting emotional journey each lesson.

I do some judging but I'm still kinda slow. Judging makes you think and focus hard on the game. It's probably the best way to gather pure knowledge about fencing. It's so analytical. When you're bouting it's less cerebral. Much of the time it's action and reaction.

3-1: Lesson #36: Full Lesson, Full of Baloney

I show up after missing Wednesday's lesson and my private. Nestor wonders if I'm OK. I guess I've become a fixture. If I don't show, my Club calls Missing Persons.

After warm-ups, I pair with Green Legs and we dash through stuff. Nestor and I have a lesson during class and then another for almost 30 minutes after. He tells me that he's giving me more time, but not to tell anybody. I wonder if he thought I was losing interest or something because I skipped the private? Nothing could be farther from the truth! These fencing lessons are now a cornerstone in my life!

I fence Mark in class. Mark's moniker is now "The President" because he is, in fact, the president of his junior high class. I guessed that. I tell him that that figures because he's always telling us what to do. He laughs and I whip his butt.

Van Dyke has shown the most improvement of all in the last four to six weeks. I have bouts with him and Green Legs after class and my lesson with Nestor. My match with Green Legs is epic, as usual. I do well enough, but I have a tendency to get hit with simple attacks, which means I'm setting myself up. Either not retreating or parrying. And thinking too much about offense.

Van Dyke judges, and I end up getting pissed about calls. By the end of the bout (which I lose) I'm angry. Dan is happy with the intensity and I simply nod. I force myself to shake Van Dyke's hand. I can't believe what a sore sport I can be sometimes! I guess I still want to win every time and the intensity of a good bout takes me over the top. I can only hope that everybody understands. It's hard to be nice when you wanna win!

Afterward I tell Kathleen about it and she exclaims, "It's supposed to be fun. What's the matter with you!" And I really don't know. Can't be a saint every day.

3-3: Lesson #37: Chums

There's a regular crew as of late. Green Legs, Van Dyke, me and the guy who came back after a six-week layoff. Since he works with

Kathleen [my wife] shows up and watches me beat Tattoo (yeah!) and get beat by Green Legs. Afterward she tells him that I lie awake at night and mutter, "I gotta beat Green Legs!" over and over. Very funny.

gems we call him the Gem Meister.

We all get along. The truest test: They ignore my outbursts. Always a strong indicator of a healthy relationship.

After warm-ups, I pair off with the Gem Meister who asks me to lead the way. This is the first time I've coached anybody in fencing class. I'm flattered. I've always felt that everyone respected my progress but no way would anybody listen to me. (Of course, I've never tried to impart my meager store of fencing wisdom, thinking that it's too soon and that I'm somewhat unworthy.)

We work on the basic drills. It's the only time you can perfect your form. When you're bouting it's something else entirely. For example, you don't think about holding your head up when the action starts. Because I'm coaching, I must focus on the drills of my partner. Heck, half the time I'm daydreaming during my drills.

My work with Nestor is high spirited and friendly. He likes to thwack the top of my mask every time he's displeased with my performance and that cracks me up for some reason. It's like a big tree crashing in on the roof. It really rings my ears. As usual, half of what he says floats on by, but I've come to understand that that is how it is with me and that I'll probably pick the stuff up subconsciously (strange but true).

In bouts with Green Legs and Van Dyke I win and lose, in that order, but it seems we're after something else tonight ... like getting it right! We try to judge better and work on new moves. Now as I write this, it's obvious that we should be bouting with learning in mind, but it isn't always like that. In the heat of the match everyone wants to score touches. It's only natural.

Van Dyke's victory tonight was his first against me, and I could tell he was charged about that. I told him that he shouldn't be surprised because he has improved so much in the last few weeks.

I also fenced Nestor and that's always a gas. It's more fun to fence better fencers. Makes you try your best. He wins of course, but I score twice. It's my defensive game that needs help (along with everything else!).

3-5: Lesson #38: Sick

I'm struck with the latest illness but come to class to get out of the house. I fence surprisingly well and wonder if being a little out of it might help. I make good decisions and place my point about as well as I ever have. My private with Nestor is intense as usual. And darn if I can remember the stuff we went over. The thing is, once I'm exposed to the new stuff, it gets filed away in muscle memory and usually pops out during a bout.

3-8: Lesson #39: Bellowing

Some drills with Bill Gates Jr. and a quick turn with Nestor. Working on low line things and attacks in opposition (I think). It's a sequence of drills that we've been working on that Nestor says is coming out during my mini-bouts. Lessons are free flowing without labels. Reaction and response. Getting the sword hand and blade to enter new territory. It's not important to attach names.

The bouts are great. I beat Green Legs 3–zip (Yeah!) and get two touches on Nestor before he prevails (Nestor fences us all and we all get two touches before he wins, so I don't feel too giddy with my scores). After class Green Legs wants a rematch (of course) and beats me 4 to 2. He scores off direct thrusts while I'm stupidly standing there and making other mistakes that are all too typical.

I get hot and dispute the calls (as usual) and Van Dyke (who always seems to be the judge when Green Legs and I bout) is a little put out with my complaints. I try to smooth it out by saying I'm only worked up because of the match (which is true ... I always get worked up with Green Legs, and he with me) but Van

> He likes to thwack the top of my mask every time he's displeased with my performance and that cracks me up for some reason. It's like a big tree crashing in on the roof.

Dyke doesn't buy it. I think his feelings are a little hurt and maybe I should tone it down. Of course Danny is fine with my bellowing (because he won) and just laughs. I think we understand the intensity between us OK, but Van Dyke might be taking it personally. I gotta do something about that.

3-10: Lesson #40: Low Point

Monday nights are particularly cool because a regular crew shows up. We all get along and look forward to the lesson and especially the mini-bouts afterward. I get really worked up during a match with Green Legs, however, and bounce my foil off the floor. It feels so good to let it out and everyone knows I'm only blowing steam, but I know I'm getting out of control. Nestor quietly lets it be known that I've reached rock bottom with my outbursts.

I decide to keep the huge dent in my guard to remind me of my temper problem. I won't last long in this sport unless I chill.

3-12: Lesson #41: Super Session

I didn't get home until 9 o'clock. After the regular lesson, I had my private and a series of matches with everybody including Nestor, whom I beat twice in five-touch bouts. Of course, he was fooling around with stuff, trying to get me to do this and that as a coach. So it wasn't like I really defeated him or anything. But Wow! It was exciting all the same!

3-15: Lesson #42: The Slows

Not with it today. Had a good drill with Mark The President but nothing crossed over to the bouts. I lost to Green Legs after another titanic struggle and then I got whipped by The Preacher. I was angry about Green Legs (not at him, but with my performance), because I repeated the same mistakes (not retreating, running into his blade, etc.). I was happy for The Preacher, though, because the guy never wins and today he beat three of us. Good for him!

3-17: Lesson #43: Not Tonight, Thank You

The regular Monday night crew of Green Legs, the Gem Meister, Van Dyke and I cheerfully sail through the drills and then pair off. The Gem Meister works on his form, and later Van Dyke and I get into some made-up things where we each try to out guess-each other.

During the bouts I defeat the Gem Meister as well as Green Legs and show pretty good form. I pace myself, parry and retreat properly and attack wisely. I also keep my head. It helps that Nestor is judging. No lousy calls.

At class end, Green Legs wants a rematch, but I say I'm tired (I really am) and slip away. This, of course, (and to everyone's amusement) pisses him off.

3-19: Lesson #44: Dueling with The Prez, Drilling Till I Drop

Wednesdays are long nights because of the private lessons with Nestor. Combined with the ever heated mini-bouts, this makes for a terrific workout. The President and I bout up a storm and he cracks me up. With everyone else he hardly tries, but with me he's on it. A knowledgeable and intelligent fencer, he can do it when he's in the mood and apparently he gets charged up with me. Nestor says he puts out the effort with people he likes.

Afterward, Nestor drills me until I nearly drop. We go over a bunch of things that remain nameless and are only a blur in my mind. This used to bother me (way back when) but now I know that it's muscle memory that counts. The object is to drill, drill, drill! and to let it sink in subconsciously. The new skills will pop out during the bouts. At one point near the end I'm actually swaying like a drunk and quietly whimpering from the effort. Undeterred, Nestor says, "One more drill!" and makes me stagger/laugh through one more forgettable exercise.

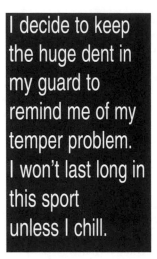

I decide to keep the huge dent in my guard to remind me of my temper problem. I won't last long in this sport unless I chill.

And to think at one time I thought fencing was for wimps!

3-22: Lesson #45: Another Flare Up

We take turns judging and bouting. When it's my turn to judge, it all goes straight to hell. I really don't like to judge because I don't have the memory or the analytical ability to do it well. I'm slow. I'm also blind without my glasses. Anyway, there I am trying to call a match and after awhile everyone starts to butt in and make the calls. I mean, it was like I wasn't even there. I try to laugh it off, but I finally get irritated and tell them all to get bent.

Well, that goes over like a lead balloon. The class goes silent and mopey but I could give a hoot. I finish up and stomp away, madder than hell. I sorta powwow with Nestor for a minute or two and as I cool off I start to feel bad (as usual). So I get back into the mix (I can't go away all pissed off).

Then I have an absolutely epic bout with Green Legs. We fence to a 4–4 tie before Dan lands the final touch. It's the cleanest, most well defined match we've ever had. Every hit is indisputable and most of the time we call our own touches. It's a fine way to end an otherwise miserable day.

3-26: Lesson #46: I Guess It's OK

Things are moving along but uneventfully. Although I agonized over my behavior the last two days, nobody says anything about it and I'm embraced by the crew. It's a fine thing that they can overlook that.

I bout with Nestor a couple of times and he shreds me with his fast hands and feet. He can parry at the last second (which makes him almost unbeatable) and his ripostes are like lightening. The only times I can score are when he fools around and I make the direct attack, or if he guides me through a hit (wanting me to try something we've gone over in class). But it's pure pleasure to bout with him all the same.

3-31: Lesson #47: Hellsapoppin!

Class is jammed tonight. Maybe eight new faces. About 20 total. Nestor is jazzed. He likes a full lineup. I pair off with one of the new guys who has good form (he keeps his back foot flat during a lunge ... perfectly flat) and is very quick. He's fenced before but a little hazy on some of the technique. We go over the stuff and he picks it right up. Sharp as a tack.

The mini-bouts are surprising. The new guys kick butt! Dan gets creamed by my new guy and Van Dyke is wasted by some fellow from Tennessee (!). The first guy is fast and low (he's short), and Mr. Tennessee is textbook perfect. Obviously, these guys aren't beginners.

Eventually, I face off with my "student" and before I know it he has me down 3–zip. He makes me attack and catches me flatfooted every time. I can't penetrate. I'm a little flustered after the final hit and pretend to take a swing at him. "No more coaching for you," I say and I'm only half joking.

I have to leave earlier than usual. I take a final look back, and it's an awesome sight. There are 20 people out there drilling or bouting. Most of them are from our foil class (the rest are veterans or team players who show up to practice). It's a very full house and it's rockin'! Obviously, the good word is out. Cabrillo is the place to throw steel. Man, the floor is swaying from 40 thundering hooves and with all the crashing blades it sounds like hell-sapoppin.

The last thing I see is Danny Green Legs challenging the guy who beat him earlier. Good old Green Legs. Just can't take it lightly.

Well, neither can I.

Chapter Twelve

A Brief **History**

From Clubs to Cleavers

The history of fencing is largely a history of weapons (and mankind's consistently mean habit of whaling on one another). Early man used clubs and later developed stone axes. The ancient Greeks and Romans developed the use of short swords, spears and shields.

By the Middle Ages swords were heavy, double-edged offensive weapons that took two strong arms to cut, slash and bash. Much too clumsy to parry with (defensive sword skills had yet to be developed), defense was left largely to body armor. Sword fights with these monster blades were tactically simple: He who landed first with the most muscle won.

Thrust, Punch and Kick

The development of gunpowder in the 14th century turned the world of war upside down. Heavy armor and broadswords gave way to guns, cannon and a more mobile approach to combat, which included the skillful use of lighter swords. As swords became lighter and more manageable, swordfighting skills were more easily developed and the true evolution of the blade began. After 1500 swords gradually became precise thrusting tools versus the old cut and slash.

Gentlemen wore the lighter swords for offensive fighting and used their cloaks and daggers for defense. Thrown into the dueling mix were kicking, punching and wrestling. It wasn't all that pretty to watch until much later on. (You know, I research this stuff and write it all down, but can you imagine arming yourself with a sword every day just to walk down the street? And *using it* every time some guy spit on your shoe?)

Fencing Goes Uptown

Eventually, guilds or schools of swordsmanship were formed throughout Europe (first in France and Italy). Swordsmanship became an important skill for noblemen (some ladies, too) to acquire. Each school developed its own special style of fencing and tried hard to keep it a secret. Footwork and lunge techniques were invented and refined. Modern fencing positions were developed including the use of the weapon as a defensive tool (the name "fencing" comes from the word and concept of "de*fense*").

A Classy Way to Go

Dueling was all the rage in 16th and 17th century Europe and weapons became lighter still. Outcomes of duels were considered God's Will. They became a dangerously popular way to settle many disputes including those concerning personal honor. In fact, so many bluebloods were killed as a result of dueling that it was banned in France and England (to no avail).

The practice of dueling throughout these years was a strictly mannered affair. It's from dueling that modern fencing has acquired the traditions of custom, officiating and tactics (as well as the notion that fencers are a touchy, high-strung, aristocratic lot).

French and Italian Influences. Henry VIII?

The rivalry between the French and Italian schools of fencing sparked the first international fencing tournaments. The French brought a cerebral approach to the sport and the Italians a more physical outlook. Fencers from France and Italy went to Germany and Great Briton to spread the good word. Although partial to the ax, King Henry VIII gave the sport its official blessing and send-off in England.

Bloodsport to Funsport

Over the last 200 years the French developed the modern sports of foil and epee.Their mark on the sport is obvious as nearly every fencing technique has a French name (French is fencing's official language).

Italy and Hungry developed saber over the last 100 years or so and it's the youngest of the three fencing arts. The practice of dueling for blood ceased in that time span, and the popularity of fencing as a healthy sport has grown immensely in its stead.

Fencing was included in the first Modern Olympic games of 1896 and is generally considered one of the most creative, intellectually stimulating and pure athletic pursuits in all of sports.The United States Fencing Association estimates that there are more than 150,000 fencers in America today.

A Fencing Timeline

1190 BC: Evidence indicates that ancient Egyptians may have fenced a bout or two in between pyramid projects.

1286: Contrary to popular belief, swordfighting wasn't always a classy thing to do. Swordfighting schools are banned this year in London. Such guilds are considered a hotbed of villainy and probably were.

1500s: The first generation of fencing masters (mostly Italian) make their mark. Fencing is taught as a "science" to budding duelists.

1530: Achille Marozzo develops the first system of swordplay.

More 1500s: The popularity of dueling and the development of fencing are riding a wave. Fencing becomes an important pursuit of noblemen. The strict and formal courtesies of fencing develop. The rapier appears on the scene and in time becomes the overwhelming choice of European duelists.

1599: England's George Silver publishes *Paradoxes of Defense*. The book defends cutting weapons and knocks the rapier. The English still consider the thrusting approach to swordsmanship highly suspect, but the Brits come around eventually.

1600s: The invention of firearms replaces the sword as a basic weapon. Fencing begins to develop as a pursuit unto itself.

Early 1600s: Italy's Camillo Agrippa simplifies fencing techniques through logic.

1650: The small sword is the clear favorite of serious swordsman.

1600-1780: More than 40,000 noblemen are thought to be killed in sword fights.

1700s: Lighter swords are developed along with a linear approach to fencing (before fencers commonly moved every-which-way). The foil is developed as a safe(er) training weapon. The science of swordplay can be explored and expanded like never before (since one can now learn and live to practice it). Fencing advances as a science and masters become highly respectable. Fencing schools are filled with young men of breeding.

1750: La Boessiere invents the first fencing mask although not in general use until much later. (It's a he-man thing: only pussies wear masks! Facial scars earned in bouts are considered badges of honor in many circles.)

1763: Domenico Angelo publishes the *School of Fencing*. Angelo is also thought to have developed the the riposte.

Late 1700s: Swords give way to handguns for personal combat. The sword is no longer an integral part of a gentleman's everyday dress. Fencing is practiced more and more as a sport although dueling is still prevalent.

1800s: Fencing comes into its own as a high sport. This is the era of great fencing masters and minds. Saber and epee are introduced to fencing competition. The fencing mask is commonly used by midcentury. This encourages fencers to use a freer, more natural style of fencing.

1891: The Amateur Fencers League of America is founded (later to become the United States Fencing Association.)

1896: The first Modern Olympics includes fencing.

1900s: Can be considered the age of fencing competition.

1913: Federation Internationale d'Escrime (FIE) is founded in Europe and standardizes the rules for international fencing competition.

1930s: Epee uses electric scoring systems to keep track of touches. Foil follows suit in the 1950s and saber plugs in during the 1980s.

Glossary

Absence of Blade: When swords aren't in contact.
Advance: Stepping forward.
Angulation: Creating an angle between the wrist and the weapon in order to make a hit.
Appel (a-pel)***:*** Slapping the floor with the ball of the foot.
Attack: The initial offensive action. In foil and saber it's made by extending the sword arm and continuously threatening an opponent's target area.

Balestra (ba-less-tra)***:*** A jump and lunge.
Beat: A preparation. A sharp slap against an opponent's blade in order to deflect it or to coax a desired response.
Bib: That part of the mask that protects the throat.
Bind: A taking of the blade. The taking of an opponent's blade diagonally from high to low line and visa versa.
Broken Time: A deliberate pause made during an action that is normally made in one movement.

Ceding Parry: A parry made by giving way to a taking of the blade.
Change of Engagement: After both blades are engaged or in contact, a blade is taken over or under the other blade and re-engaged on the opposite side.
Circular Parry: Deflecting an attack by circling an opponent's blade with the sword point. Also counter-parry.
Compound Actions: Two or more actions performed as one continuous action.
Compound Attack: An attack composed of two or more actions.
Compound Riposte (rip-ost)***:*** A riposte composed of two or more actions.
Conventions: The rules governing foil, epee and saber fencing.
Coule (koo-lay)***:*** Grazing down an opponent's blade with an extended arm maintaining constant contact.
Counter-Attack: An offensive action made into an offensive action.
Counter-Disengagement: An indirect attack made by deceiving an opponent's change of engagement.
Counter-Parry: Same as a circular parry.

Counter-Riposte: A riposte following the successful parry of an opponent's riposte or counter-riposte.
Coupe (koo-pay)***:*** Same as a cut-over.
Croise: (kwa-zay)***:*** A taking of the blade. The taking of an opponent's blade from high to low and visa versa on the same side.
Cut: A hit made by the cutting edge of a saber.
Cut-Over: A simple, indirect attack made by passing the blade over an opponent's point.

Derobement: Evading an opponent's attempt to beat or take the blade.
Disengagement: A simple, indirect attack made by passing the blade under an opponent's point.

Engagement: When swords are in contact.
Envelopment: A taking of the blade. The taking of an opponent's blade that finishes in the original line of engagement.

False Attack: A lunge that purposely falls short in order to yield a response.
Feint: A false attack intended to deceive.
Fencing Distance: The distance necessary to reach an opponent with a lunge.
Fleche (flesh)***:*** A dramatic, falling-forward method of making an attack.
Foible: That part of the blade near the tip.
Forte (fort)***:*** That part of the blade near the guard.
French Grip: A relatively straight and simple sword handle.
Froissement (froys-ma)***:*** An attack on the blade. The beat and press combined.

Lunge: The most standard method of attack.

On Guard: A fencer's ready position.
Opposition: Holding or resisting an opponent's blade.
Orthopedic Grip: A sword handle shaped to fit the hand and fingers.

Parry: The act of deflecting an opponent's blade.
Piste (pist)***:*** The fencing strip on which opponents fence.
Preparations: Actions which prepare the way for a final attack.

Includes footwork, attacks on the blade and takings of the blade.
Press: A sharp push on an opponent's blade.
Priority: Relates to the right of way rule in foil and saber. The fencer whose sword arm straightens first and threatens the target area has right of way until his sword is parried or beaten out of line.
Prise de fer (pree-de-fair)***:*** Taking of the blade. These actions include opposition, bind, croise and envelopment.

Redoublement: A renewal of attack by arm or blade movement against an opponent who doesn't riposte.
Remise (rem-ees)***:*** A renewal of attack in the same line without withdrawing the arm.
Reprise (re-pre-z)***:*** A renewal of attack after returning first to on guard.
Riposte (rip-ost)***:*** The offensive action taken after a successful parry.
Right of Way: See Priority.

Second Intention: An action made to draw a particular response.
Semi-Circular Parry: The deflection of an attacking blade by drawing half circles from high to low and visa versa.
Simple Attack: An attack with only one movement or action.
Simultaneous Hit: When opponent's attack and hit each other at the same time. In foil and saber no hits are scored. In epee, both fencers receive a point.
Stop Hit: A counter attack. An attack made into an attack.
Stop Hit in Opposition: A stop hit which deflects an opponent's blade.

Taking of the Blade: See Prise de fer.

Resources

United States Fencing Association (USFA)

National Headquarters
One Olympic Plaza
Colorado Springs, CO 80909-5774
Phone: (719) 866-4511
Fax: (719) 632-5737
General e-mail: info@USFencing.org
usfencing.org

Fencing is full of great people who love their sport, and like all truly passionate sportspeople, they will gladly lend a hand. It's one of the wonderful things about fencing, in particular, because the circle is so small and chummy. No need to feel timid.

Fencing Magazines

American Fencing
This is *the* major mag. It's put out by the USFA and covers the whole enchilada. For information call or write the USFA.

Fencers Quarterly Magazine
(formerly Veteran Fencers Quarterly)
A true fencer's publication and on the cutting edge.

848 South Kimbrough
Springfield, MO 65806
417-866-1370
editor@fencersquarterly.com
www.fencersquarterly.com

TV

Watch the best fencing in the world during the Olympics. This is still the ultimate showcase for talent in this sport.

Movies

Master of Arms Buzz Hurst's top five list:

The Three Musketeers (1974)
Scaramouche (1952)
The Adventures of Don Juan (1949)
The Mark of Zorro (1940)
The Duelists (1977)

Bibliography

Alaux, Michel. *Modern Fencing.* New York, NY.: Charles Schribner's Sons, 1975.

Amateur Fencing Association. *Fencing.* London, England.: A & C Black Ltd., 1994.

Bower, Muriel. *Foil Fencing.* Madison, WI.: Brown & Benchmark Publishers, 1993.

de Silva, Henry. *Fencing.* Wiltshire, England.: The Crowood Press Ltd., 1991.

Evangelista, Nick. *The Art and Science of Fencing.* Indianapolis, IN.: Masters Press, 1996.

Garret, Kaidanov, Pezza. *Foil, Saber, and Epee Fencing.* University Park, PA.: Pennsylvania State University Press, 1994.

Pitman, Brian. *Fencing.* Wiltshire, England.: The Crowood Press Ltd., 1988.

Shaff, Jo. *Fencing*. New York, NY.: Atheneum, 1982.

Index